BALL, BAT AND BISHOP

Ball, Bat and Bishop

THE ORIGIN OF BALL GAMES

Robert W. Henderson

Foreword by
Leonard Koppett

UNIVERSITY OF ILLINOIS PRESS

URBANA AND CHICAGO

First Illinois paperback, 2001
© 1947, renewed 1975 by Robert L. Henderson
Reprinted by arrangement with the proprietor
Foreword © 2001 by the Board of Trustees
of the University of Illinois
Manufactured in the United States of America
P 5 4 3 2 1

⊗ This book is printed on acid-free paper.

Library of Congress Cataloging-in-Publication Data
Henderson, Robert W. (Robert William), b. 1888.
Ball, bat and bishop : the origin of ball games /
Robert W. Henderson ; foreword by Leonard Koppett.
p. cm.
Originally published: New York : Rockport Press, 1947.
With new introduction.
Includes bibliographical references (p.) and index.
ISBN 0-252-06992-7 (pbk. : alk. paper)
1. Ball games—History. 2. Baseball—History. I. Title.
GV861.H4   2001
796.3'09—dc21   00-067239

TO LUCY

Contents

List of Illustrations

ix

LIST OF ILLUSTRATIONS

xi

Foreword to the Illinois Paperback
Leonard Koppett

IF Robert Henderson had simply expounded his theory, so impressively researched and reasoned, that all modern hit-the-ball games derived from ancient religious rites and evolved through recent centuries, it would have made a significant impact on social historians and other small groups with specialized intellectual interests. But because he also demolished the Doubleday myth, which was then the accepted myth about how American baseball originated, he gave birth to the practice of serious treatment of baseball history and, in due course, to the world's increasing fascination with it. Exploding the Doubleday myth was the necessary precondition—and model—for all subsequent studies of baseball's true history and development.

Few of those deeply involved with baseball in the middle of the twentieth century—journalists, fans, operators—really believed the story that someone named Abner Doubleday had "invented" baseball in a place called Cooperstown in the year 1839. But baseball authorities were devoted to it nonetheless, promoting it extensively and convincing the general public of its authenticity. They went so far as to celebrate 1939 as the centennial year of "America's National Game" and even opened the National Baseball Hall of Fame and Museum in that lovely but virtually inaccessible village in upstate New York where baseball was born.

What Henderson spelled out in *Ball, Bat and Bishop* not only made it impossible to keep elaborating this wholly fabricated tale but set in motion the search for reliable (i.e., documented), reasonable details of every aspect of baseball's past. The material always existed, but only after Henderson put the Doubleday myth to rest did others begin to mine it.

That was not Henderson's main purpose in writing the book, however. A high-ranking official of the New York Public Library, he was also the official librarian of the Racquet and Tennis Club of New York. The tennis family of games was his chief interest, and the club's archives provided him with much of the data from which, over a period of thirty years, he developed his concepts about ball-game origins. Devoted to research rather than controversy, he set out to deal with three thousand years of human social history. Still, he found the baseball situation was too tempting to ignore, a sitting duck for anyone aiming for an authentic depiction of the past.

No other professional team sport of the 1920s, 1930s, and 1940s had such exposure and so avid a following as did baseball. Football, basketball, and hockey were in their formative stages, soccer was "foreign," and the entire universe of entertainment offered little competition. Only the World Series, a heavyweight championship fight, the Olympics, a few college football games, and a handful of traditional horse races were "big events" as far as the public and the media were concerned, and all but baseball (played and recorded every day for six months) occurred sporadically. Baseball was king to an extent that later generations can no longer imagine.

Ball, Bat and Bishop, not widely circulated when it was first published in 1947, took a few years to filter through the consciousness of a new generation of baseball researchers. Once it did, by the middle and late 1950s, the Doubleday myth could no longer be taken seriously by anyone, no matter how hard baseball's commercial operators tried to cling to it. Today's incredibly rich (and still growing) field of baseball history owes its beginnings to Henderson's thoroughness in following up his first love, the racquet games.

Symbolic truths do not depend on factual data, and in its own way the Doubleday myth served a purpose, much like George Washington's cherry tree caper, Nero's fiddling, and King Arthur's court. As a repository for baseball's spiritual history, Cooperstown is as good a place as any. Once established, it has become irreplaceable.

For those who care about what "really" happened—and when and how and where and to whom and with what sort of interplay with other forces—which is to say, for historians and those who read their work—Henderson's modest little book has proven to be the acorn from which baseball's historical tree—nay, its forest—eventually grew. Re-reading it in the light of all the information we have gleaned since makes it all the more impressive and, in its own way, delightful.

Acknowledgments

THE AUTHOR's interest in the history of ball games arises out
of his duties as Librarian of the Racquet and Tennis Club of
New York, where he gathered the data upon which this book
is based. Appreciation is expressed to the Board of Governors
of the Club and to the Committee on Library and Art for their
generous support and continued interest for over thirty years.

Many members of the staff of The New York Public Library
have given valuable aid: Miss Romana Javitz of the Picture
Collection, Mr. Nathan Schwartz of the Photographic Service
Department, Mr. F. I. Avellino of the American History Division, Dr. Frank Weitenkampf, whose stimulating criticism has
been most helpful, and many others.

For the privilege of reproducing illustrations we are indebted to The Clarendon Press for cuts from *The Romance of
Alexander,* Oxford, 1933; to the Pan American Airways System
for the Chichen Itza photograph; to The American Museum
of Natural History for the Aztec Ball Game from the *Codex
Florentino* and to the Bodleian Library, Oxford, for cuts from
Douce MSS 135 and 162.

ACKNOWLEDGMENTS

Thanks are due to Will Irwin, whose long-standing interest in the Origin of baseball makes his gracious Introduction to this book very appropriate, to Mrs. Geo. D. Huntington, of Grosse Pointe, Mich., and last but not least to my wife, Lucy, whose sympathetic interest, gentle encouragement and patient forbearance have made the writing of this book a happy experience.

Introduction

THE Duke of Wellington said that the Battle of Waterloo was won on the playing fields of Eton. So for that matter was the aerial Battle of Britain a century and a quarter later. But in this condensed parable, Wellington seems to have been the first to note and record the influence of sport on the character and achievements of the English-speaking peoples. Out of competitive athletics, with their emphasis on physical courage, on instant decision and action, on "standing the gaff," we developed efficiency in battle—a sharper efficiency, when it came to the supreme test, than that of the Germanic peoples who, long scorning sport as a waste of time, regimented their boys and trained them solely in the technique of fighting. Those aviators of Britain who by their split-second perception of an opening and their instantaneous translation of thought into action, whipped the Führer's air fleets in 1940, had learned the trick not on the drill-ground but in competitive sport. Rudyard Kipling momentarily denied his own philosophy when he wrote scornfully of "the flannelled fools at the wickets, or the muddied oafs at the goals."

This applies not only to the archaic—one hopes the dying—

human habit of killing other men in masses, but to our success as colonizers and mariners. Wherever circumstances required quick, instinctive action in emergencies, firm and noble endurance of pain and hardship, coolness in face of danger, the ability to throw into the balance the last ounce of physical and spiritual energy, the pioneer in a strange and lonely land, the English or Yankee skipper navigating far seas in a cockle-shell, had in his background a boy's world or a racial history which developed and exacted these very qualities.

Yet in face of these facts, our social historians have paid little attention to sports. Mr. Henderson is a pioneer when in this book he contributes his ton of soil to fill that gap. He has traced the evolution of games played with a ball from that time in the dim beginnings of recorded history when the priests of faiths now dead took hold of them and developed them as religious rites. He has gone on to the brief period when the living religion of Christianity borrowed some of these non-essential rites and to the present when the boy who kicks a football or catches a baseball does not suspect that he is honoring the dead Osiris. It is just as well that the Puritans of the seventeenth century did not know this; else to the offences which they charged against sport they would have added idolatry!

Mr. Henderson does not venture into the dim beginnings of ball games. He is too careful an historian to mix facts with conjecture. But anyone who has observed anthropoid apes in a zoo has probably noted that in one of his playful frenzies a chimpanzee will pick up some small object and throw it. He is not aiming at anything in particular. He is just enjoying the exercise. As man developed, he learned to control this faculty and to use it in hunting and fighting. Then, presumably, a cave-child, imitating in play the work of his elders, caught a thrown oak-gall or apple between his palms and enjoyed the sensation. That satisfaction of muscular desire is a large part of the pleasure in all modern ball-games—the drive whistling from a clean stroke of the club or the racquet, the pitch plopping snugly into the mitt. City clerks, throwing and catching in the street during the noon hour, are not merely practicing. They are having fun. "Playing catch" is the parent of almost all ball games. And it must have flourished for ages before some shrewd genius of a priest saw the opportunity to increase attendance at services by injecting into them a touch of muscular paganism. What the hierarchies of heathendom contributed was team work.

Doubtless the popular appeal of this book will lie in the later chapters, wherein Mr. Henderson comes to modern times and traces through original sources of information the evolution of baseball. The "Spalding" report on the invention of baseball, as accepted by our sports writers for the past forty years, came near to proving the cynical old adage that a lie or fallacy well stuck to becomes history. For a time, it seemed to the writer of this introduction, that only Mr. Henderson, he himself and a few professional players like "Hank" Gowdy spoke out against the well-exploited legend that the game of baseball—name and all—was invented at Cooperstown, New York, in the year 1839 by Abner Doubleday, later General Doubleday of the Civil War. In the end, even the standard reference books accepted the Doubleday theory. That this fallacy well stuck to did not become history is mainly due to Mr. Henderson. The Spalding Commission had the money and the time to make a scholarly investigation and arrive at a verdict on the basis of the evidence. That was not their method nor their intention. Ignoring the records then known, including Jane Austen's reference to English baseball written in the late Eighteenth Century, they started a hunt for proof that some American invented the game "without aid or consent of any foreign nation," as the Free Silver faction used to say. When they stumbled onto Abner Graves, the sole prop of the Doubleday theory, their hearts must have leaped. He came from Cooperstown, New York. And from his "memory" of events some sixty or seventy years gone by, he declared that of his own knowledge Abner Doubleday had invented the game, lock, stock, barrel and name, at Cooperstown in 1839. Mr. Henderson fails to note one fact about this testimony which seems most significant to me. Graves testified that, in the game as Doubleday taught it to his admiring townspeople, the defending team put out a runner not by touching him with the ball as we do today, but by throwing it at him and hitting him. In 1839 the children of Britain, and probably of the United States, had been playing that very game with soft balls of wound yarn for more than a century—and calling it baseball.

But the Spalding Commission, dazzled by this confirmation of their prejudices and the advertising value in Doubleday's name, did not know enough about the subject to perceive this contradiction. Forthwith, they reported that Doubleday alone fathered baseball and—taking cognizance of certain ugly rumors to the contrary—that any resemblance to any other game was "purely coincidental." As our text books in geometry used to say, Q.E.D. At about the time the Spalding Commission finished its work—the early years of this century—I was interviewing on my own account veteran professionals like Arthur Irwin and "Slow ball" Martin. None of them went back in memory to the 1840's when the Knicker-bocker Club introduced modern baseball in New York. But they had all talked to these pioneers. Their opinion on this subject was almost unanimous. From the old game then called "rounders" in England, and baseball—later "Boston baseball"—in the United States, the modern game had evolved as the result of a seemingly minor change. Some one had conceived the idea of putting out the runner by touching him with the ball, held in the hand, instead of hitting him with it. That made it possible to use a hard ball, like the one used in cricket, without danger of committing involuntary homicide or mayhem. So baseball became not a child's game but a man's. Who had that idea? No one knows for certain. Mr. Henderson is too conscientious an historian to advance tradition as proof. But when a tradition comes through many channels, it should have some standing in court. So another fact merits recording. Most of these old-timers, repeating what they have heard from their elders, attribute the idea to Alexander Cartwright, leading spirit of the Knickerbocker Club.

Possibly this change was a kind of composite performance. It seems likely that many a parent or teacher, noting the joy of the little boys in throwing the ball at the runner as hard as they could, with consequent black eyes and bloody noses, said, "Why not just touch him with it?" and enforced his new rule with a leather strap. For often these boys employed very substantial materials for their balls. In treating of Indian games, Mr. Henderson records that men of the tribes which lived on the shores of Lake Erie used the gristle that grows in a sturgeon's head. My father was born in that region in 1844 and grew up there. He told me that he and the other white boys carved their baseballs out of that very same material, which is at least as heavy as hard rubber and less elastic. It seems possible that the boys of Erie, Pennsylvania and the surrounding towns had adopted perforce the idea of the "touch" long before Mr. Cartwright organized the Knicker-bocker Club.

This introduction has edged away from Mr. Henderson's book, as such writings will. Coming back to it: the early critics of the Doubleday tradition base their skepticism mostly on observation and common sense. What they lacked was a thorough investigation undertaken in the scientific spirit. Mr. Henderson has supplied that. From his favorable position in the New York Public Library, one of the largest collections of books, documents and old periodicals in the United States, he has followed his gentle hobby for a quarter of a century. I will not anticipate him, except to say that he presents proofs which reduce the fame of General Doubleday to its proper stature—that of the man whose resolute fighting spirit saved the Union Army on the first day of the decisive battle at Gettysburg. The rest was a bubble, now pricked.

WILL IRWIN

BALL, BAT AND BISHOP

1. Mythical Origins

GAMES today are pastimes undertaken primarily for pleasure. Most of us play games of various sorts: lawn tennis, baseball, badminton, bowling and such like "for the fun of it." While educators encourage athletic activities for their value as body builders, and golfers look for the beneficent results of a day spent out of doors, if not for the development of a few business contacts, the major purpose in the minds of the millions of people who play games is that of personal enjoyment and relaxation.

This attitude does not go very far back into history. It is far from being true as to the origin of the various games now played with bat and ball. As we delve back into the records of ancient civilizations, we find that folk customs and religious ceremonies, undertaken not as idle pastimes, but as grim supplications to various deities, are the roots from which our modern sports have sprung. Strange as it may seem, the lawn tennis championships played at Forest Hills or Wimbledon, the English pastime of cricket and the popular American game of baseball are merely vestigial remains of religious

3

rites of ancient times, designed to influence the pagan gods that they might make the crops to grow, and so ensure the continued existence of a grateful people.

The origin of ball games in general has puzzled many scholars, and their conclusions have been more suggestive than conclusive. It has been claimed that the games stemmed back to ancient rituals, efforts to control the seasons magically, supplications to agricultural deities. Prof. F. P. Magoun of Harvard has shown the association of football with traditional customs. W. Brand Johnson asks the question: *"Is Football a survival of magic?"* and submits much evidence in support of the theory that it is. But no one has yet presented the story of tennis, baseball or any other ball game, showing a step by step development of the game from a rite to a pastime. It is the purpose of this book to show that all modern games played with bat and ball descend from one common source: an ancient fertility rite observed by Priest-Kings in the Egypt of the Pyramids.

Perhaps the oldest of all folk tales is the story of the warfare between Horus and Set. Osiris, the mythical king-god from whom the Egyptian dynasties sprang, was pre-eminently a god of agriculture. In those beginnings of civilization, long before the scientific spirit had revealed to mankind the mysteries of the processes of nature, primitive man stood in awe and wonder when, as each spring returned, the earth sprang to life again. But their awe and wonder were considerably tempered by fear and dread lest the annual miracle should fail to occur. To make sure about it they sought the aid of their gods by whatever means they could. To Osiris they looked for aid, for he was the god of all things that grew: it was his favor that made possible the growth of the wheat in their fields and the fruit on their trees.

Osiris and his consort Isis exercised magical influence upon the growing crops. But evil forces symbolized by the wicked Set had to be reckoned with. Set was the god of darkness, the negation of all growing, living things. After many crafty efforts Set managed to kill Horus, son of Osiris and Isis, and to hide his body in an attempt to prevent his life-giving influence. The distressed mother Isis, after long, agonizing search, found the body, only to have Set once more rob the grave. This time he severed the body into many sections and secretly buried them in many places. Once more the bereaved Isis went up and down the land searching for the dismembered body of Horus. As she went she wept copiously, thus watering a parched earth. Finally the quest of Isis was successful, the parts of Horus' body assembled, whereupon he ascended to the Egyptian Heaven, safely beyond the reach of Set.

The folk tale is the most primitive form of education, or, if we may use a modern term, propaganda. It evolved slowly, painstakingly, over long periods of time, transmitted verbally from generation to generation, not to amuse four-year-olds, but to convey to the adult mind the concepts, beliefs, *mores* of each civilization. It was the means whereby a people could be knit together in a feeling of unity of purpose in their common endeavour to perpetuate themselves.

In the story of Horus and Set we find the earliest traces of a dualism so characteristic of the early Egyptians. It taught the belief that their welfare somehow depended upon the goodwill of a supernatural power whose aid was necessary to overcome the malign influences of an opposite and contrast-

5

ing power. This power they imagined in the little understood, unharnessed forces of nature: the winds and storms of all seasons, but particularly in the unfruitfulness of the dormant winter period.

This two-sided aspect of nature must have been very real to the Egyptians, for they emphasized it to a remarkable degree. They paired all kinds of things in their daily living, in their political organization, and in their religious ceremonies. Egypt was not just "Egypt," but "Upper and Lower Egypt," and the title of the King was expressed by the double term. The King was twice crowned. His palace was in two parts; he had two treasuries; there were two temples, each with two High Priests, and even their religious vessels had two spouts. It is plainly evident that this curious organization of their whole life was considered essential to the well-being of the community.

This distinctive feeling of the early Egyptians of the dual nature of the universe was so strong that its influence can scarcely be over-rated, for it spread practically through all primitive civilization. It is even found amongst the Indians of North and South America, where vestiges survive to this day in a variety of tribal customs. In practically all early cultures we find traces of religious rites, all practiced in the springtime of the year, in which contrasting forces are pitted dramatically one against the other.

Naturally, since the gods were involved, religious ceremonies show the greatest evidence of this dualism. In Egypt the rituals took the form of the conflict between Horus and Set, or rather between the dying winter and the oncoming spring. It might have been simple at the beginning to dramatize and stage this oldest of folk tales, and let the ceremony go at that. Indeed, from such dramatic presentations in Egyptian temples it has been claimed our modern theatre has come. To the priestly class belonged the privilege of conducting these life-giving rituals, and we must remember that the kings were also the top-ranking priests. But such important matters could not be restricted to a select few. Judging from the large numbers who eventually participated in these activities, it became essential to enlarge them from the exclusive prerogative of the priesthood to include as many of the common people as possible. And so we find forms of ceremonies, such as a dramatic combat between various groups. The contests were, of course, mock combats, but when one's life depended upon the outcome, there could be no trifling. The people engaged in the fights in all earnestness, and there is abundant evidence that the blows were struck with deep religious conviction. The deeper the conviction, the harder the blow, and many and serious were the injuries inflicted.

2. Mock Combats

Mock combats of many kinds were common in antiquity, still very much in evidence during the middle ages and survive even today. Sir J. G. Frazer in his famous *Golden Bough*, A. H. Krappe in his *Science of Folklore*, F. M. Cornford and other anthropologists have noted many instances of these customs. There were contests with sticks and stones; sometimes stone throwing only; sometimes a tug of war between contending forces and occasionally races. In certain places the ritual combat was accompanied by a wedding, held in a ploughed field, a custom replete with symbolism related to the idea of fertility.

One of the earliest of these contests took place annually at the Temple of Papremis, in Egypt, where priests and people enacted the traditional drama. "More than a thousand" men, votaries of the god Osiris, lined up at some distance from the Temple. With them they had a previously prepared image of Osiris in a gilded casket, which in turn rested on a four-wheeled cart. The object of the group was to "rush" the image of Osiris through the Temple door and, to aid them in this, each man held a hefty wooden club. But in front of the door of the Temple, in strong defensive array, and also armed with wooden clubs, awaited an army of priests, ready to prevent the expected onslaught. When all was ready, the image of Osiris moved forward, the eager votaries stormed the gates and clubs were wielded with vigor. "There was hard fighting with clubs," the story reads, "and heads were broken." But no lives were lost. This annual custom at the Temple of Papremis is of particular interest in that it shows a breaking away of the agricultural rites from the exclusive priestly-aristocratic classes, a process of democratization which was to be soon paralleled in ancient Greek culture.

A further development of the Egyptian mock combat is described by Herodotus. In his travels, about the year 450 B.C., he observed a springtime custom of a Libyan tribe, the Aures. First, all the maidens assembled for a beauty contest. The winner was arrayed in Corinthian armor, including a helmet. Then, mounted on a chariot, protected from the sun by a Grecian panoply, she headed a gay parade along the shore of Lake Tritonia where the event was held. It was a great day for the young lady selected. But soon her troubles began! The maidens were divided into two groups, with the beautiful winner undoubtedly at the head of one, given a supply of sticks and stones, with which they proceeded to fight one another, "thus (as they say) honoring after their people's manner that native goddess whom we call Athene. Maidens that die of their wounds," continued the historian, "are called false virgins," a rather sad end to a nice spring festival.

Herodotus was careful to mention that although the occupation of Asia Minor by the Greeks influenced the type of armor worn by the maidens (and it must have been very necessary!), in earlier days it was Egyptian, thus connecting the

9

custom with the dualistic rites of ancient Egypt. In all probability the honoring of Athena by the Greeks was associated
with the ceremony of the *Three Sacred Ploughs* by which the
signal for seed time was given, and the ceremony of the
Procharisteria at the end of the winter, when thanks were
given for the germination of the seed, both obviously of importance to an agricultural people.

In ancient India the ritual combats varied from village to
village. In Kumana, for example, a custom known as the
Bagwah was a heaving of stones at opposing groups, while
the *Barra* was a ceremonial tug of war between two villages.
Throughout Northern Africa the contests were fought between
villages, between tribes, but also between married men and
bachelors, or married women and maidens.

And so on, throughout all primitive cultures, examples could
be quoted of these ritualistic, dramatic conflicts, always super-
vised by medicine man or priest, actively engaged in by large
numbers of people, all with one purpose: to supply man's most
fundamental need—food.

One other primal instinct is closely related to the search for
food, that of self-preservation, which fortunately is not limited to the individual, but is apt to be expressed in terms of
tribe or race. With the insistent demand for food is the instinctive need for children. Life is a struggle for proteins and prog-
eny. It was this latter instinct that led to the introduction into
the springtime festivals of the little understood folk customs
such as the *Saturnalia*.

Although the ritualistic dramatizations and folk customs we
have described were undoubtedly agricultural and the idea of
the fertility of the soil their main purpose, it was not long

10

before the idea of human fertility and perpetuation of the human race became so intermingled with the original idea that it became impossible to separate the two. After all, an abundant food supply to maintain a population is but half the story.

Gradually the observances took on characteristics which have long puzzled historians; only within recent years have they been understood. Such springtime festivals of the ancients as the *Saturnalia, Lupercalia, Dionysiac Rites* and the earliest forms of the Feast of Purim were periods of license and debauchery by modern standards, times when morality and law seem to have been temporarily abandoned. Writing as early as 1499, Polydore Vergil considered the Easter ceremonies of the Church to be a survival of the Roman *Bacchanalia*, the *Lupercalia, Saliorum Ludi* and *Hilaria*, all festivals during which the peculiar, temporary inversion of both rank and morals occurred. Peter Roberts, writing in 1815, noted the carry over of these festivals into the *Twelfth Night*, the pre-Lenten period of foolery of the early Church, when masquerading through the public streets was a favorite amusement. He suggested that since "all were celebrated at this season of the year, it may probably be thought that the season in general was one of mirth, and the festival of the Church a true portrait of the pagan." But Roberts did not grasp the real significance of the pagan practices.

Usually there was a divine pair: Haman and Vashti, Mordecai and Esther, Marduk and Ishtar, later a divine king who had his female escort, with whom he performed the necessary ceremonies. All forms of sexual license, gross in the extreme, were freely practiced by all and sundry, while wine

11

flowed freely. Processionals through the streets gave fresh impetus to the wild orgies. At the end of the period, however, the person who acted as king forfeited his life—a stiff price to pay for a brief period of merriment—after which the usual routines of life returned.

Why such a period of license? Why did not the ancients protest against practices which to us are so repulsive, and to them at normal times were equally foreign? As Frazer says, "The contrast between the summer and winter, or the life and death which figure in effigy or in the persons of the living representatives at the spring ceremonies of our peasantry, is fundamentally a contrast between the dying or dead vegetation of the old, and the sprouting vegetation of the new year —a contrast, I may add, which would lose nothing of its point when, as in ancient Rome and Babylon and Persia, the beginning of spring was also the beginning of the new year."

But the value of the rites was not only agricultural: they had a deeper social significance. Man, to survive, must not only have a supply of food, but himself must survive racially. It was this thought of race survival that induced the orgiastic ceremonies. In short, as Prof. Belknap has put it, "primitive man awakened spring by imitating it. The ritual acts of the winter festival must have recalled and reawakened that inner vitality of which the same acts, as spring rituals, were direct expressions. And in this momentary awakening men must have found assurance of the continuity of their own vital energy through the depression of the winter, and promise of personal resurrection. This, and the sustaining hope which faith in magic gives for a rebirth of vegetation are the only values which we as rationalists can allow to the winter ritual. But these were great values in the childhood of civilization."

Today our Carnivals and *Mardi Gras* are feeble vestiges of these lusty religious rites.

The *Saturnalia* and other harvest festivals are sometimes referred to as "December liberties," which seems puzzling at first, but the relationship between the December festivals and the springtime fertility rites is not difficult to establish. Frazer states that "The resemblance between the *Saturnalia* of the ancients and the Carnival of modern Italy has often been remarked; but in the light of all the facts we may well ask whether the resemblance does not amount to identity. . . . The Carnival is held in March. . . . Now, if the *Saturnalia,* like many other seasons of license, was observed at the end of the old year, or the beginning of the new one, it must, like the Carnival, have been held originally in February or March, at the time when March was the first month of the Roman year. . . . In rural districts the ancient festivals continued to be celebrated at the ancient times, long after the change in the calendar had shifted the official celebration of the *Saturnalia* in the towns from February to December. Later, Christianity, which struck at the root of official or civic paganism, has always been tolerant of its rustic cousins, the popular festivals and ceremonies which, unaffected by political and religious revolutions . . . have been carried on by the people from time immemorial, and represent in fact the original stock from which the state religions of classical antiquity were comparatively late offshoots. Thus it may well have come about that while the new faith stamped out the *Saturnalia* in the towns, it suffered the original festival, disguised by a difference of date, to linger unmolested in the country."

Frazer comes to the conclusion that festivals of the type of the *Saturnalia* were at one time held all over the ancient

13

world, from Rome to Babylon. "Such festivals seem to date from an early age in the history of agriculture, when people lived in small communities, each presided over by a sacred or divine king, whose primary duty was to secure the orderly succession of the seasons, and the fertility of the earth."

3. Ball and Team

H. J. MASSINGHAM has suggested that in the ritualistic grouping into two parties, dramatizing the conflict between winter and summer, we have the original division into "teams," that is, two groups competing one against the other for supremacy, but in a nonwarlike manner. The opposing sides in the tribal ceremonies made natural teams long before the ball made its appearance and became the center of conflict as the symbol of fertility. As Massingham expresses it, "No sooner are we back in antiquity than we find it was the teams that made the game. Wherever it was played among peoples who retain or retained traces of the archaic culture which once overspread the world, we are made aware that it was a formal and sacred rite, conducted between two sections of the community whose political existence depended upon the division. . . . Out of this dualism arose the ball game which, in the Pacific and in Morocco . . . was a ritualistic, spectacular exhibition of this dual grouping in action."

But this association of ball games with a nation's food supply is by no means new. Polydore Vergil, in 1499, produced the earliest "first facts" book, in which he set out to establish who invented things—a small encyclopedia. In this he credited the Lydians with the invention of ball games, but he states that they did this not as a pastime, but because of a shortage of food, quoting Herodotus as his authority. Herodotus does relate that in the reign of Atys, son of Manes, "there was a great scarcity of food in all Lydia." Divers plans were devised by many men to meet the situation. Finally they rationed themselves: on alternate days they ate or refrained from eating. "Then it was they invented the games of dice, knuckle-bones and ball, which they played on the foodless days" to help them to forget their hunger. The famous historian was correct in associating the ball games with hunger, but he did not have the facts quite straight as we now understand them. The connection of the ball with the food supply was not as a game, but as a symbol in the dualistic rites we have described. Incidentally, this seems to be the first instance of rationing.

So much for the origin of the team. Just how and when the ball was introduced into the tribal combats is difficult to determine. The origin of the ball itself is lost in antiquity. A spontaneous origin appears at first to be a reasonable guess. It is natural to throw things—stones, apples or any round object, and what more natural than to throw back? And what more natural than that some form of ball game should be developed? Strangely enough, there is little evidence to support this theory. In the Scriptures, for example, replete with references to ancient Hebrew customs and folk-lore, there is but one mention of a ball, and that only a vague figure of speech.

Massingham discards the theory that ball games sprang up spontaneously as innocent amusements. "Inference from the total cultural evidence of the past shows," says he, "on the contrary, that the ball game must have been a royal prerogative. It was first played not by common folk, but by kings, and divine kings at that, and only by ordinary men who were delegated by the priests to take part in the holy function." He further insists that "the antique ball game was more than a prayer for rain: it was an actual means of not only decanting the clouds, but for making the crops to sprout, the flowers to shine . . . and the earth to renew her winter weeds outworn. . . . The ball game was a religious ceremonial instituted by ancestor king-gods who were credited with miraculous powers over nature. The divine Pharaohs were rain makers and the solar and fertility deities were legion." The French anthropologist A. Moret bears similar testimony.

There are various theories as to how the ball was introduced as a "bone of contention" between the opposing sides. There is no doubt as to what it symbolizes: the idea of fertility. We have mentioned the temporary king who held sway over the springtime festivities only to forfeit his life as a sacrifice at the conclusion of the ceremonies. Eventually this person was replaced by a puppet king. Perhaps one of these kings, shrewder than his predecessors, found a way to wriggle out of a tight situation and successfully recommended a substitute at the psychological moment. The puppet then represented the ancestor king-god. But a puppet is a clumsy affair as a center of a free for all fight. Too many people could lay hands on it at one time and pull it apart. What then was the most essential part over which the fight could be waged with finality? Massingham again provides testimony that the head, symbolizing the mummified head of Osiris, the mythological god of agriculture, was selected as the most potent part of the puppet. In the ritual of mummification the head was always regarded as the most important part of the body, and

17

numerous head cults have sprung up because of this ancient mythological belief in the potency of the head.

Indeed, in modern times the cult of the head is by no means extinct. Every boy has been thrilled by stories of the head hunters of Borneo and similar tales. A recent traveller in Egypt described an interesting ceremony in which a survival of the ancient beliefs strongly supports the idea of a fertilizing head. Barren women, desirous of bearing children, retire to an ancient tomb. Seven times forward and backward they step over the mouth of the shaft leading to the subterranean burial chamber. Then certain charms are placed on the ground, and seven times each woman passes over them, forward and backward. The charms are four in number: one, a cat; the second, a scarab; the third, a mummiform divinity; the fourth, a representation of the head of Isis, sister-wife of Osiris. Once more the ritual is repeated; the third and last time over two heads, one a well preserved mummified head and the other a skull. This ritual was reputed to aid barren women to bear children. The emphasis on the use of the heads, especially the image of the head of Isis, surely indicates a belief that has existed for centuries in the efficacy of the head as a fertilizing agent, a belief which may well have caused struggles for an object of such potency and thus became the earliest form of the ball.

A remarkable survival of this idea was observed by one of Stanley's pioneer officers in Central Africa, on the historic search for Livingstone. It reveals beliefs closely allied with ancient head cults. When it was considered necessary to make a human sacrifice, an unfortunate slave was firmly tied to stakes in a sitting posture. Then a flexible sapling was planted in the ground in front of him, from the top of which was suspended, by a number of cords, a bamboo ring. The pole was bent over and the ring put around the slave's neck, kept rigid by the tension of the sapling. Then came the ceremony, dancing and drunken mimicry, the climax being reached when the executioner, with one stroke of a keen-edged weapon, sliced the head from the body. The tension released, away flew the head, catapulted for some distance, to fall amongst the awaiting tribesmen. A ghastly, bloody struggle followed; for the rest of the day the head passed from man to man, until one retained it in undisputed possession. Thus is established the right to be recognized as the bravest man in the village.

Other theorists interpret the ball as a symbol of the sun—the source of all life—and many writers could be quoted in support of this point of view. But whatever may have been the origin of the ball, the evidence is overwhelming that in ancient Egypt and throughout the adjacent lands, the ball represented the idea of fertility, the life-giving principle. Whether this particular symbolism derived from the head of Osiris, or from the sun, the central thought is the same. In all probability the two ideas are inextricably combined and the answer to the question, "Which is correct?" would be "Both." Osiris was the god of agriculture, but many have identified him with the sun. Nevertheless, as we shall see, the form in which the ball ceremonies dominated ancient cultures, and even those of more modern times, was as head cults, where the magical properties sought resided in the head of a Divine King, or later in the heads of enemies of the tribe.

One of the earliest representations of a ball ceremony is found on the north wall of the main chamber of Tomb 15 at Beni Hasan, which was built before the year 2000 B.C. It shows semi-nude women, in pairs, one woman mounted on

19

the bent back of the other, throwing balls. Since at a much later date we know of naked women engaging in ball "games" designed to encourage rainfall, it is probable that this ancient Egyptian ritual had a related purpose.

Another representation of a ball ceremony inscribed in Egyptian tombs occurs about the year 1500 B.C., on the eastern wall of the entrance hall of the Shrine of Hathor, in the Temple of Deir-er-Bahari. Thothmes III holds in his right hand, ready to strike, a wavy olivewood stick. In his left hand, ready to throw into the air, he holds a ball. Facing the king stand two priests who appear to be catching the balls. Opposite, at a distance, stands Hathor, who has been identified with Isis. The inscription tells us that the ceremony is in honor of Hathor, and that "the enemies are struck before them," a nice figure of speech symbolizing the defeat of the evil forces of the non-productive winter season.

The ball, of course, was known to the ancient Greeks and Romans, and many have assumed that our ball games derive from this source. But such is not the case. According to Herodotus the ball was introduced into Southern Europe by the Lydians when they crossed the Mediterranean Sea. In Greece physical exercise was deemed of importance in the cultivation of the body beautiful, and the ball was used in such exercises. In Rome also ball games were strictly of a calisthenic nature, being played for the purpose of conditioning the body and the training of athletes. In Roman baths and gymnasia were specially constructed "ball rooms." Various kinds of ball were used: a leather covered handball; a heavier feather-stuffed ball, and a solid wooden ball. The uses to which the Greeks and Romans put the ball, however, were strictly of the medicine ball variety. The ball was thrown from player to player for exercise. There were no competitive ball games with teams or players opposing one another.

But one exception must be noted: the game of *episkyros*. In this game a number of young men gathered in a large arena covered with sand or dust. A line was drawn across the center of the playing field, and at equal distances from the center line boundary lines were marked at each end of the field. A ball, called a *skyros* was placed on the center line, and each team gathered on its own boundary. At a signal both sides rushed to gain possession of the ball. *Episkyros* is quite different from all other Greek or Roman ball practices, and is seldom mentioned in ancient literature, but it is so characteristic of the ball ceremonial contests that it must bear some relation to them. The Lydian origin suggested by Herodotus may be correct.

4. Islamic Rites

ALTHOUGH the dualistic agricultural rites originated in ancient Egypt, they appear to have spread rapidly to Arabia and Persia, and became part of their culture so early that it is impossible to determine the dates. Our present knowledge of the rites is such that it would be nearer the truth to call them Egyptian-Arabic-Persian on ground that they were indigenous to the larger area.

With the coming of Mohammedanism and its doctrine of one God, the ancient Egyptian dualistic fertility rites took on a new lease of life. So deeply rooted had they become in the lives of the peasants that any attempt to eradicate the older religious customs associated with the many tribal deities would have been a well-nigh impossible task. Seemingly, at least as far as the agricultural purposes of the ceremonies were concerned, the pagan idea permeated the Mohammedan culture, rather than being replaced by the newer religion, and the Mohammedans adapted easily, if not avidly, the springtime rites. Many writers have described customs throughout northern Africa, clearly indicating that they became part and parcel of the new faith.

Indeed, in northern Africa, it is possible to trace the same practice through many local changes, across many centuries. We have already mentioned Herodotus who, about 450 B.C., saw the springtime customs and suggested that they were of Egyptian origin. More than seven hundred years later St. Augustine noted the seasonal occurrence of the festivals. The good saint must have been a little proud of his ability as a preacher. He recounted how each springtime the people under his charge at Caesarea horrified him with the severity and cruelty of their customs. The people divided themselves into two groups, and literally killed each other with sticks and stones. Instead of virgins, as in former days, kinsmen, even brothers, fought against one another in furious combat. But, claimed St. Augustine, by the sheer force of his eloquence, he had been able to dissuade the Caesareans from this brutal practice, despite the fact that it had been handed down to them by their fathers and ancestors of generations gone by. Alas, the cessation was but temporary, for about one thousand years later, Leo Africanus saw the same customs which St. Augustine thought he had abolished. By the time of Leo Africanus, however, the ferocity of the games had considerably diminished.

These stick and stone combats at an early date must have centered about a round object similar to a ball, for as time went on the ceremony slowly resolved itself into what appeared to be a free-for-all hockey match. In the year 1921 another traveller reports how, in the evenings during the spring festivals, there was played at Menea and elsewhere in Algeria a game called "koora," or "ball," which very closely resembled hockey and which, the writer notes, was "of great antiquity." E. Doutté, in his book *Merrakech*, in 1905, also speaks of these "games," and states that they are played *only* in the Spring. Westermarck gives examples of many related customs which varied from place to place, but all with the same intent: they were rain ceremonies in which were acted the strife between the winter drought and the springtime rains. In one tribe, two or four naked women play a kind of hockey with large ladles; in another tribe sticks were used instead of ladles, and in yet another place good old women play at ball when rain is desired. In one village something resembling a football match is played, after which a ewe is draped with a woman's shawl. Again, at another village, it is the custom for men and youths in spring to play at ball with sticks as a means of producing rain. Westermarck insists that the essential function of playing at ball is to bring about a change in the weather through the movements and changing fortunes of the game.

5. Polo

ACCORDING to the *Encyclopedia Britannica* polo is the most ancient of games played with stick and ball. It also states that the earliest records are Persian. But the problem is to decide the time when a folk custom of distinctly religious connotation became secularized into a game, for polo has a definite relationship to the old Egyptian-Mohammedan ball-fertility rites.

The word *polo* is from Tibetan *pulu*, meaning ball, which might suggest the Tibetan or Chinese origin of the game. But all authorities agree that polo is of Persian origin, after which it quickly spread eastward through Turkestan, Tibet, China and even to Japan.

Granted a Persian origin, there are many theories concerning the invention of polo in that country. Perhaps the most colorful theory is based on the story in *The Arabian Nights: The Tale of the Wazir and Sage Duban*. According to this oriental romance, the King was stricken with a dread disease, a situation which called for an unusual remedy. The physician, so the story goes, fashioned a bat with a hollow handle, into which he packed certain unnamed drugs. Then the King

was instructed to get up on his royal horse and swat a ball
with the medicated stick. This the King did with much energy.
Soon he worked up such a perspiration that his skin, hot and
damp from the exertion, absorbed the healing qualities of the
drugs, and, presto! he was in the best of health. So polo was
invented, say some of our historians. But *The Arabian Nights,*
pleasant and entertaining though it is, cannot be taken as
history, and the story itself makes no such claim.

Accounts of ball games in ancient Persia and neighboring
countries are many, and although we must rule out the picturesque Sage Duban as the inventor of polo, to the fact that
many of these early games were played on horseback lies the
rightful claim that polo originated in Persia. But one important point to remember is that there exists no *contemporary*
record of the oldest of these ball customs. The earliest record
of "polo" in Persia is to be found in the works of Al-Jahiz,
who died in A.D. 869. Like the earliest part of the Old Testa-
ment, these Persian histories describe events which occurred
hundreds of years before the authors were born. The accuracy
of the statements, therefore, needs considerable checking, for
of course the writers colored their work by their own points of
view, and in the light of extremely primitive historical scholar-
ship. Nevertheless testimony is abundant, and one may be
sure of the historicity of the ball customs, if not of the details.

These early "games" have one puzzling feature: the large
number of contestants, sometimes as many as a thousand on
a side! The great historian Tabari, writing about the year
900 A.D., relates how, in the year 230 A.D. Ardashi I proved
the legitimacy of his son, about which there had been some
doubt, in a kind of "trial by battle." The battle in this case
was a "game" of polo. "Then Ardashi ordered the boy to be

groomed for presentation at court with a hundred, or according to others, with a thousand other boys of his age. These should all be led in at the same time, care being taken that no distinction be discernible in their dress, height or manner. The old man carried out the order. No sooner did Ardashi look upon the boys than, without the slightest hint or suggestion, he delightedly recognized his son among them. He next commanded that they be led into the court of the palace. There they were given hooked staffs, and they played ball while the King watched them."

In the year 1435 the Spanish traveller Pero Tafur described a game sponsored by the Sultan Barsbai, Malik al-Ashraf: "That day the Sultan (of Egypt) dined in the field, and afterward they played a game that is customary there, in this manner: they place a ball in the center of the field, and some thousand horsemen, more or less, take up their position on one side, and they draw lines on either side in front of them, and each has a mallet in the hand, the handle of which is called a staff, and they all attack the ball at the same time, with intent, on the one side, to drive it across the line, while the others seek to do the same on their part, and those who succeed in driving the ball across the line are the victors. That day one of the players tried to hinder the Sultan's son, and he took out his sword, and tried to kill his opponent, and there was a great commotion until the Sultan came up and parted them."

By the year 1170 similar traditional ball games had spread to Byzantium, or Istanbul, as it is now called, where they took the name of *tzycanisterium*, which was also the name of the place where it was played. It is described by Cinnamus, as translated by Prior: "But the winter was passing away, and

27

when the murkiness had cleared off, it being customary from of old for kings and kings' sons to devote themselves to some moderate exercise. . . . Some young men divide themselves into two equal parties, and throw one another a ball made of leather, of about the size of an apple, into such level ground as, after having distinctly measured it out, they think may suit them so as to have the center equidistant from each. After this ball, lying in the intermediate space between them, they rush to meet one another at full gallop, each brandishing in his right hand a staff proportionally long, and ending abruptly in a broad curvature, the middle of which is divided out with gut-strings dried gradually and plaited into one another, net fashion. Each side now makes it a point of emulation to get ahead and transmit the ball to the other goal, which of course has been marked out for them from the first. For when the ball has been so driven by the staves as to have arrived at either goal, the victory thereby falls to that side. Such is the character of the game, slippery in every way, and dangerous; for it is necessary for one who takes part in it to be always leaning backward, and twisting from side to side, and wheeling his horse in a circle, and turning his horse in every direction, and to be jerked about in as many kinds of movement as the very ball itself may happen to be."

Cinnamus implies that this game was confined to men of rank, and Constantine Porphyrogenitus agrees with this: "You will find another double course of the same length as that of the north, and parallel with it, that too extending to the Royal Palace, down to which it was an established custom for kings and the sons of wealthy people to play ball on horseback." Du Cange, the famous medieval scholar, writing in 1668, links *tzycanisterium* with the game of *chole,* or *la soule,* "only that

Thothmes III in symbolic ball
ceremony in honor of Hathor, *c.*
1500 B.C.

Ball game of Egyptian Women.
From the Tomb of Beni Hassan.

Ball player, England, c. 1350. *Part of Great East Window, Gloucester Cathedral. The head was damaged by Cromwell's Roundheads.*

Ball players, England, 14th Century.
From a Misericord in the Choir at Gloucester Cathedral.

it is played on foot. On certain fête days, and generally on
the festivals of the patrons of the villages, peasants invite their
neighbors to a match. To play it they throw a large ball into
a high-road between the confines of two villages, and each
party drives it with his foot till the strongest brings it home,
and in this way carries off the victory." All accounts of
tzycanisterium, or *chicane*, as it was called in France when
it was played with sticks, agree that large numbers played on
each side.

Why such huge "teams" in these accounts of "polo"? As
many as a thousand played on a side. By the time of Cinnamus, in the middle ages, the earlier customs were settling
down into "exercises," but in Persia, when the Egyptian rites
were being translated into traditions adapted to a nation of
horsemen, the "players" did not participate in the activities
as games and sports are understood today. Rather, at least in
the earlier periods, the opposing sides were merely observing
the traditional dualistic ceremonies, which reverted either
consciously or unconsciously to the ancient fertility springtime rites. It was customary for large numbers to take part
in these ceremonies, either in the form of combats, or in other
places as funeral lamentations, or delirious jubilations, ceremonies which called for the magical rebirth of the earth's
vegetation, and which can be traced back to very early times
in the texts found in the pyramids.

As was the case in other "games," as they became the common heritage of the people their religious significance gradually disappeared and a meaningless "custom" survived or a
skillful game developed. Polo travelled to China, where it was
known about 600 A.D., but at that time, one historian claims,
it was considered to be a revival of football! The earliest men-

tion of polo in China is by the poet Shen Chuan Chi, who died in 713 A.D. Modern polo, rediscovered by the English in India, was first played in England in 1869, and now is a popular, if expensive, game in most parts of the world.

6. Christian Ball Ceremonies

THE game of polo, as we have seen, was perhaps the first secular form of the old pagan religious rite. In the excitement of the combat the religious significance slowly disappeared, while interest as a pastime increased. To the peculiar use of the horse in the ball rites must be assigned the development of polo in Persia. But let us see what happened in the less spectacular customs observed in other places.

As the Mohammedans travelled east and west, the fertility rites went with them, and certainly the popularity of the springtime customs was very great throughout Northern Africa. In the eighth century the Moors crossed the Mediterranean, rapidly spreading throughout Spain to Southern and Western France. For many centuries the Moors ruled in Spain, and although at first they were exceedingly tolerant towards Christianity, it was but natural that the religion of Mohammed should slowly but surely permeate the daily life of the people of the Spanish Peninsula. Of course there was some opposition, but as yet Spain had by no means been Christianized. In larger cities ecclesiastical organizations flourished, but the rural districts were largely pagan. In fact, a majority of the population, especially those holding political responsibility, espoused the faith of their conquerors. In Aragon, for example, the Spanish Mohammedan Beni-Casi ruled, it is said, "supported by a loyal population of Mohammedans."

With the Islamic culture of the Moors came also their closely related folk-customs, including the folk-fertility springtime rites which they had absorbed from the Arabians. So marked had this custom become, that a description of the rites in Northern Africa would equally apply to the customs of Spain.

Lady Wentworth suggests that certain ball games, especially tennis, came over to Europe with the Moors, and that the Greeks probably imported their ball games straight from Persia or Egypt as early as 490 B.C. "In Persia," she said, "there were two sorts of ball games, one called *savlajan,* played with a stick curved or hooked at the end, which was obviously the origin of polo. The other, *chigan,* sometimes spelt *Tchaugan,* was played with a shorter and stringed racket, and must have been the origin of the French *chicane,* or *Jeu de Paume* (Tennis), and the Greek game *Tzganisterium.*" What crossed with the Moors into Spain was not the *games* of ball, tennis or polo, but the Mohammedan rites modified by the customs of different localities through which they had passed.

It was quite natural that the ball rites of the Moorish invaders, regularly observed in the spring of the year, should become associated in the minds of the people of Spain with Christian Easter festivals, for they were practiced at the same time of the year, and both symbolized the idea of rebirth. That the association of the two ideas, or more probably their confusion, resulted is not surprising, when it is recalled that Christianity was not at that time firmly established in Spain. Undoubtedly in some places the spread of the Mohammedan custom synchronized with the growth of the Christian ritual. At a time when Spain was steeped in ignorance and barbarism, in superstition and prejudice, the Moorish *marabout* who competed with the Christian priest, had come to exercise a more potent influence over a credulous people than a tribal chief, or even an Arab governor could ever hope to acquire. The illiterate people, hearing both the priest and the *marabout*, would have difficulty in separating the two ideas; would more easily combine them, and this they undoubtedly did. Once firmly established in Spain, the Mohammedan customs spread into southern and western France, and it is here that the two customs, pagan and Christian, were finally fused into one.

We may go further, and claim that the association of the pagan fertility ball-rite with the Easter festivals was deliberately fostered by the Church, for its usual policy was to adapt to, or incorporate into its ceremonies those pagan customs which it found too firmly established to be uprooted, or to be susceptible of adaptation.

As early as the year 400 A.D. Saint Augustine advocated that "Christians ought not to reject a good thing because it is pagan. God is the author of all good things. To continue the good customs that have been practiced by idolators, to preserve the objects and the buildings which they have used is not to borrow from them; on the contrary, it is taking from them what is not theirs and giving it to God the real owner. Such things may be consecrated directly for His worship, or indirectly in honor of the saints."

And so heathen gods were supplanted by Christian saints, and pagan temples converted to Christian usages. An excellent example of this sagacious and subtle policy is given by the Venerable Bede. He quotes approvingly a letter written by the Pope Gregory in 601 A.D. to a missionary Abbot named Mellitus, in which he stated that "it is impossible to efface everything at once from obdurate minds," counselled moderation, and advised the Abbot not to destroy those heathen temples which were well built, but to cast out and utterly destroy the idols therein, and to convert them "from the worship of devils to the service of the true God." He also advised that sacrifices once made to idols should in future be offered "to the Giver of all things."

This policy of converting heathen practices to Christian purposes was continued by Pope Boniface IV, so that Anastasius his librarian could write: "Has not everything in Rome, formerly heathen, now become Christian? Have not all the temples of the false gods been changed into Churches of the Saints? Has not the Temple of Apollo been converted into the Church of the Apostles? Has not the Temple of Castor and Pollux been made the Church of Cosme and Damien?"

So general was this practice of adaptation that Sir Isaac Newton observed that "the heathen were delighted with the festivals of their gods, and unwilling to part with these ceremonies," and that the Church, "to facilitate their conversion, instituted annual festivals to the Saints and Martyrs: hence the keeping of Christmas with ivy, feasting, plays and sports came in the room of the *Bacchanalia* and *Saturnalia;* the celebration of May Day with flowers in the room of the *Floralia;* and the festival of the Virgin, John the Baptist, and the divers apostles in the room of the solemnities at the entrance of the sun into the signs of the zodiac in the old Julian calendar."

Similar testimony is given by Jacob Grimm, the German scholar: "The festivals of a people present a tough material, they are so closely bound up with the habits of life that they will put up with foreign additions if only to save a fragment of the festivities long lived and tried. In this way . . . the Anglo-Saxons down to a late period retained the heathenish Yule . . . As faithfully were perpetuated the name and in many cases the observances of Midsummer. New Christian feasts, especially of Saints, seem purposely as well as accidentally to have been made to fall on heathen holidays. Churches often rose precisely where a heathen god or his sacred tree had been pulled down, and the people trod the paths to the accustomed site; sometimes the very walls of the heathen temples became those of the Church, and cases occur in which idol images still found a place in the wall of its porch, or were set up outside the door, as at Bamberg Cathedral there lie Slavic heathen figures and animals inscribed with runes."

"Thus," Dexter concludes, "heathen buildings were adapted to our Christian uses, and heathen ritual incorporated into Christian worship. The incorporation into Christianity of some of the good things in heathenism (and heathenism had its good points) was the policy of the Church. The utter destruction of everything pagan was not practical, nor was it attempted. So heathen fanes became Christian temples; some heathen rites, Christian ritual."

That the pagan fertility rites in which the ball was featured was one of the practices adapted by the Church, changed slightly in meaning, and converted to Christian use is beyond doubt, for the ball gradually passed into Christian ritual as a symbol of the Resurrection, and became part of the Easter observances of the Church. As the idea became assimilated into the various folk-cultures of Europe, it assumed a large variety of forms as it became adjusted to local traditions, but it always retained its ancient connotation of fertility. Most of these customs center around the springtime of the year, and are found as part of the Easter celebrations: many are associated with local bridal customs. Upon the adaptation of the pagan ball rite into the Easter Christian ceremonies hinges the subsequent development of the bat and ball games so familiar to us today.

It is in Southwestern France, to which the Islamic customs had reached, that we find the earliest reference to the ball as part of an Easter ceremony, and a most remarkable account it is. On Easter Day, we are told, at the services in the Church in the City of Auxerre, early in the twelfth century, it was the custom of the Dean of the Chapter and other Church officials, properly robed for the occasion, with amices on their heads, to form in a processional. Then a ball was handed to the Dean by a clerical student, after which the *Prosa* suitable for Easter day, which begins *Victimae Paschali Laudes,* was chanted by those in the procession. As they sang, they proceeded down the aisle of the Church, while the Dean, taking the ball in his left hand, danced to the rhythm of the Easter hymn. The others, skillfully moving in dance steps, swung with the music, as hand clasped hand, alternating with the ball as it was passed from dancer to dancer, all keeping in time with the organ which played the measures of the dance. After this exhausting custom the dancers were entitled to a little refreshment. Accordingly a feast became part of the official proceedings. The record states: "nor was the game of ball uncustomary in other Churches. To be sure, what was done in the Church at Auxerre was done in a more seemly manner at Vienne, in the palace of the Archbishop."

At Vienne it was the custom on Easter Monday, at vespers, while the bells were rung, for the whole assembly to come together in the Archbishop's Palace. The tables having been duly set with allspice, wine and food, a formal Easter meal was taken, after which the Archbishop threw a ball amongst the assembled people, who promptly played a game of ball. Provision was made that if the Archbishop happened to be away at the time of the Easter celebrations, he should see to it that some one in his stead threw the ball to the crowd, in the approved manner.

It was not to be expected that such unorthodox customs as the ball ceremony should pass into the Church without some protest, and indeed the staid, older priests raised strong objection to the profanation of the Easter observances by the introduction of pagan practices. The first of these conservatives was Jean Beleth, a Parisian theologian, who in 1165 went on record as opposing the ball games at Poitiers and other places. "There are some Churches," said Beleth, "in which it is customary for the Bishops and Archbishops to play in the monasteries with those under them, even to stoop to the game of ball." Then he gave his reasons: the ball games, he said, were simply the old pagan customs, when at the "December liberties" male and female slaves and shepherds were granted license, and "became in the same condition as their masters, in a common festival after the collection of the harvest. In truth," he added, "although great churches such as that at Rheims observe the custom, nevertheless it is more praiseworthy not to play."

A century later, in spite of the protests, many prelates remained faithful to the old traditions. On Christmas, or at Easter, according to local custom, Archbishops, Bishops and other dignitaries laid aside their ecclesiastical rank, and, "with their fellow servants of God, great and lowly," sang and danced and played at ball. Once more a protest was raised, this time by William Durandus, Bishop of Mende, in the year 1286. "In certain places," he complained, "in our country, prelates play games with their own clerics on Easter in the cloisters, or in the Episcopal Palaces, even so far as to descend to the game of ball, or even dancing and singing." And then he quoted Beleth to support his contention that the practice was the old pagan custom in a new Christian setting.

The testimony of Beleth and Durandus, both eminently qualified witnesses, clearly indicates that in the twelfth and thirteenth centuries the ball had found a place for itself in the Easter celebrations of the Church, and that it was a time when there was an inversion of rank, much as it had been practiced by pagan peoples in such customs as the *Saturnalia*.

7. La soule

PERHAPS the earliest form of the pagan rite, after it had
become Christianized in Europe was the traditional game
of *la soule* as found in France in the twelfth century. *La soule*
approximated very closely the old Moorish customs: there
was the same taking of sides between large groups, sometimes divided regionally and sometimes by marital condition. There was the same centering about the ball; the same
use of sticks, large, small, curved or stringed. There was the
same association of the game with the springtime of the year,
now called Easter or Shrovetide. But now we find in the observances the additional association with the Church. Jusserand's description of the game makes very clear these associations: "*La soule* although played by the nobility, by
ecclesiastics, and even by kings was by preference the
popular game. Parish played against parish, single against
married men. These little tournaments put all the country-
side *en fête*. In the evening there was drinking and dancing
and it was a time for general merrymaking, for the players
comprised all the village. It was one of those happy days
of which one dreamed long in advance, and which broke the
monotony of the workshop and field. The day selected was

frequently the Mid-Lent, or Shrovetide, that is to say, the *Mardi-Gras,* but it was often the day of the patron saint of the parish, Easter Day, or Christmas. Very rarely a day arbitrarily chosen."

Bearing in mind the fierce character of the contests in the ancient rites, engaged in by large numbers of people, we are struck immediately by the many resemblances to the game of *la soule* as played in France, and especially in Brittany, early in the middle ages. The resemblances are so great that we may claim that the game is definitely associated with the earlier fertility rites.

La soule was played with a ball driven with the foot, the hand, or sticks of varying kinds. The ball was usually made of leather, stuffed with bran, hemp, wool or some similar material. Occasionally it was wooden. The phrase *chouler à la crosse* found in a letter dated 1381 leaves no doubt as to this form of the game: it was a forerunner of the modern lacrosse. Other documents of 1361 and 1387 use the terms *ad soulam crossare* and *bastonner à la soule,* indicating forms of the game played with sticks of different shapes. In 1374 at Chauny, the game was said to have been the custom "so long ago that no one remembers to the contrary."

In some places special customs required that the ball be made in a certain manner. In Rochay, a village in Langest, the ball had to be made of black leather softened with oil. At Epinard an elaborately prepared ball was used: each quarter was of a different color, and several crosses were painted upon it. These ecclesiastical embellishments undoubtedly arose from the fact that the whole district of Epinard was owned by the Abbey of Ronceray, and hence a natural tendency to such decoration.

Records of the game of *la soule* are found in many rural districts throughout France in the fourteenth century, such as Vermandais, Bray, Vexin, Meldvis, Brie and others, where it was played on feast days such as Christmas, Candlemas, Shrovetide and Lent. Again we have the familiar division: single against married men, and parish against parish. The purpose of the game was to drive the ball as far as possible into the territory of the opposing side. At Beaufort, in Anjou, the ball had to be put into play by the newly married men with the older married men as their adversaries. The winning side achieved victory by reaching a goal set by the *Sénéchal,* an important feudal functionary. At Coriac in Auvergne, in 1450 the game was played by married men against single men. At Vexin Normand, about the year 1380, it is recorded that these games were played before the door of the Abbey of Nôtre Dame de Mortemer. At Cleville, in the district of Caen, the contests took place between two villages on either side of a dividing river, and the custom here was to present a sheep to the winning side.

There is much evidence of the severity of the game which was always a warmly contested, prolonged struggle, often bloody and sometimes fatal. In 1830 at Neufchâtel-en-Bray, while *la soule* was played "in the traditional manner, the game became so rough that a priest was struck in the face by one of the players, so as to cause blood to flow. The players were threatened with expulsion from the game." That the proximity of a priest to a game of *la soule* was no rare thing may be surmised from the *Journal* of the Count of Gouberville, who relates that a certain *curé* of Tourhaville, after saying Mass, "knocked the ball around at *choule* all the rest of the day."

41

Townsmen playing *la soule,* France, 1497.

In 1440, in the Synodal Statutes of Raoul, the Bishop of Tréguier gives a vivid description of the game: "It is decreed that these dangerous and pernicious games be prohibited because of the ill feeling, rancor and enmities, which in the guise of a recreative pleasure, accumulate in many hearts, give baleful occasion for hatreds to arise. We have learned from the reports of dignitaries of the faith that in some parishes and other places under our jurisdiction, both on feast days and others, for long time past, of certain pernicious and dangerous games, with a large ball, vulgarly called *mellat* (another name for *la soule*). It has already resulted in many scandals, and it is manifest that it will produce others, if a remedy is not found." Excommunication was threatened to all who disobeyed. The ball folk-customs must have been deeply entrenched in the lives of the people to be carried on so vigorously with so much damage to themselves, and in spite of the opposition of the Church, which, as time passed, became stronger and stronger. But they were hard to eradicate. As late as the fifteenth century these same characteristics of tribal combat, with all their ferocity, were

42

observed by the Picards and Artesiens, near the Chapel of Vauchelles-sur-Authie, in the Somme. Practically all citations show some association of the Christian Church with the game of *la soule*, or other ball games. They were played on Christian festivals; they centered around the Churches, and priests participated. A curious survival of the game at Avranches, until shortly before the Revolution, shows how firmly associated with the Church the ball rites had become. There, at the *Mardi-Gras*, the Bishop of Avranches and his canons, each armed with a *crosse*, and followed in a processional by the lower clergy and the choir, went to a beach in the vicinity of the city, near Pont-Gilbert, and there played a game of *crosserie*, a primitive lacrosse. Each volley of the ball was a signal to ring the great bell of the Cathedral. Similar events took place at Genets and on other beaches on the Bay of Mont-Saint Michel as late as the year 1840.

Another survival of *la soule* was observed at St. Cybardeaux in Charente, where the custom was still in vogue as late as 1857. On Christmas Day, each man married during the preceding year had to contribute towards a ball, which was then batted along the bank of the river. All the young people ran to capture it, struggling with one another for its possession. Obviously it must have been a rather tough pastime, but when it was all over the winner received a prize provided by those who had taken part in the game. In Morbihan, about the same time, a similar custom was prohibited on the ground that it had become too dangerous.

Historians have attempted to explain the many curious characteristics found in *la soule*. Pezron states categorically: "I do not doubt that the round ball we call *la soule* was invented by the ancient Gauls in honor of the sun, and for that reason it is thrown on high." But Gougaud adds: "Today one can decide less certainly, in the absence of other proofs, that the origin of *la soule* is as ancient as the Celts. All that can be said of the antiquity of the game is that, if we can believe the witnesses of the second half of the fourteenth century, it seems, at that time, to have been implanted in many countries for a long time."

The widespread and repeated references to the "man last married" undoubtedly have some bearing on the idea of fertility, a vestige of the ancient pagan ideology. And the intervention of the Church, so remarkably demonstrated in the above citations, can only mean one thing: the Church sought in these customs, as in so many other ways, to adapt a pagan practice to Christian purposes. Gougaud believes that "*la soule au pied* (*la soule* played by kicking the ball), as it was called in the fourteenth and fifteenth centuries, is probably the authentic form of the primitive game," and we can agree with him that *la soule* was the first form of a secularized game based on the pagan rites, after they had been blessed by the Church. It is also the parent stem from which cricket, baseball, lacrosse and other games played with bat and ball have descended. The ferocity with which the game of *la soule* was played, and the fact that so many took part, might be expected to bring up the matter of the keeping of the peace. When the crowds got going, and in the excitement of the struggle heads were broken as well as windows, who could intervene to get things back to normal, or at least place some reasonable restrictions on the wild participants? It is not surprising to find various efforts to control, if not to suppress the games. Some attempts have already been noted, but such

44

power resided in the King himself. He, in turn, handed over the delicate job to his feudal barons.

It must have been with some reluctance that the barons undertook the troublesome task of preserving order at a season when the wildest license had been customary. By way of an alibi they were forced to claim certain legal rights which gave them the authority to intervene. Thus, in their efforts to control the festivities, the barons gradually assumed certain rights, which developed into an amazing series of local customs.

As early as 1369 Charles VI of France tried to suppress *la soule* because of its dangerous nature, but evidently in 1440 it had not lessened in severity as the further restriction of the Edict of Raoul shows. Control, rather than prohibition was first attempted, as for instance in 1147, where feudal rights seem to have been established, for in ratifying a deed of gift to the Church at Beaumont, in Rouergue, the Seigneur of Trincavels specified amongst other privileges which he retained, the remission, or fee of seven balls of the largest size. In some places a vassal had annually to present a ball to the Seigneur, for it was the privilege of the Seigneur to bat the ball out, or throw it to the assembled people, on days fixed by custom. This must have been more than a formal throw, such as takes place at baseball parks at the beginning of a season, when some official starts the proceedings.

On these occasions we again find that it was the man last married who presented the ball. Other customs, more or less extravagant, grafted themselves onto this medieval "right."

Historians have claimed that the right of the monopoly of the *soule* attributed to the seigneurs was simply a police measure. The game, so popular, but so dangerous, condemned by both Church and King could but gradually disappear. The seigneurs at last cut down the ceremonies to one day each year in their efforts to suppress it entirely. In the exercise of their rights the seigneurs took some part in the games, and the ball was usually put into play by them personally, or by a representative. At Josselin the ball was presented at noon on the day of the *Mardi-Gras*, before the Cross of Martray, between two dishes, with two loaves, two jugs of wine and two glasses: quite a formal occasion. At Gué-de-l'Isle it was deposited on the seignorial pew in the Church after High Mass. The same custom was observed at Langest, by the Seigneur de Rochay. A peculiar custom, reminiscent of the *jus primae noctis,* was observed in the Chatelain of Mareuil in Berry, where, *en secondes noces* after his marriage, each bridegroom had to present to the seigneur a bat of certain length and two new balls. In La Pommeraie, in Normandy, the tenants had to supply the Seigneur de Flers with a leather ball. There is on record at Vitre, as late as the year 1580, a custom which shows to what an amazing extent the Church had given significance to the use of the ball. Here, on the Feast of St. Stephen, in a little Church dedicated to that Saint, at the most solemn moment of the High Mass, between the elevation of the Chalice and the Host, the proceedings stopped while the Seigneur, in great dignity, marched up the aisle to the altar, and laid upon it a ball. At Rochefort in Pluherlin, as late as 1554, the last man married was obliged to carry a ball to the Seigneur, and then throw it over a public oven, having one foot braced against the wall of the churchyard of Nôtre Dame de la Trouchaye. If he failed to accomplish this feat, he had to pay a fine.

8. Tennis

THE theory that the game of *la soule* is the common origin of various ball games has been generally held, and seems to be fairly well substantiated. Jusserand supports the theory in his splendid study of ball games. Barthelemey claims *la soule* to be "none other than the origin of tennis, and all those amusements in which one strikes or struggles for a ball, large or small." As to this, however, we would suggest that tennis and *la soule* sprang from the same root almost simultaneously. Polo, of course, sprang directly from the Arabic rites long before they migrated to Europe.

Most interesting of all the references to early ball games in France are those to the game of *jeu de paume,* or tennis, played in the earliest stages with a ball and palm of the hand, and in its later stages with racquets. It might be noted here that tennis, or court tennis as it is known today, is the old indoor game, and should not be confused with the modern adaptation, lawn tennis. Court tennis is played in a court shaped like a stylized cloister. The ball must travel over the net, as in lawn tennis, but may also be bounced against the walls, or from the roof of a low gallery which extends along

47

three sides of the court, much the same as the cloister in a Cathedral. The method of scoring is highly complicated. Earlier records are not always clear as to the form of the game played, but there is a close association between tennis and *la soule,* for both derive from the same source. "If batting the *soule,*" says Barthelemey, "was a popular diversion, we find it also in the higher classes of society, and even among the clergy."

The student of tennis, delving into the history of the game, is struck by the fact that the earliest players were ecclesiastics: bishops, canons and clerics, who played it in their cloistered courtyards, and even in the palaces of their cathedrals and churches. Why should this group be especially interested? Then the student notes that not only did the early ecclesiastics play tennis, but they played it *at the Easter season.* Why at Easter? It was of course another instance of the ancient pagan festival, but now scarcely recognizable, this time confined within ecclesiastical circles, and adapted to Christian usages.

It cannot be said that the game of tennis originated at any precise point of time. It was slowly developed in a process of evolution covering centuries. The earliest references to these ball games, which we have already described, cannot of course be considered as tennis, but they do show how the ball was introduced into religious circles. It should also be remembered that the racquet was not in general use until well into the sixteenth century. It is certain, however, that tennis was brought to a point in its development which differs little from the modern game of court tennis, *while still played by hand.* The thirteenth century might be considered as the period during which tennis actually became a game.

There are no records to show that tennis was played, even in the primitive form before the tenth century, but forms of the game were probably in vogue in certain cloisters and court-yards of churches and church schools in the twelfth century. These dates harmonize with the theory that Christian customs were influenced by Mohammedan traditions after the Moorish invasion of Spain.

We have already shown that in the twelfth and thirteenth centuries ball games were observed in a number of important churches, if not as part of the official services, at least closely related to them. In a discussion of the word *pila* (ball), a writer in the *Mercure de France* of May 1726, is of the opinion that the game referred to is *jeu de paume*, or tennis, and quotes in his support the *Rules* of the Chapter of Auxerre of April 18, 1396, an ordinance on the making of balls: "It was ordered that Masters Stephen de Hamello and John Clementeti, who were new stagiaries, should offer a ball (*pilotam*) on the first Monday after Easter, and it was es-tablished that the beginning of the month be set aside for the said ball (pila). This ceremony then as you see, is some-times called *pila*, sometimes *pilota*, but since that time I have found only *pilota*. They played with a ball which each new canon had to present to the assemblage so that they might exercise with it."

As embryonic forms of the game of tennis appeared, the symbolism became less marked, and more vestigial in char-acter, but some religious significance clung to the game for centuries. L'Abbé Boutillier gives a very natural explanation of the sympathetic attitude of the Church towards the social activities which accompanied the observation of its great feast days: "The joy which filled the first Christians on the greatest

49

of their solemnities, the Easter Celebration, and the reiterated invitations made to them, in the Divine Offices, to give themselves to pure and innocent joy on this holy day, those which the apostle states are fruits of the spirit, has been experienced by the great heroes of Christendom, and the most sorrowful and austere penitents, to mark this dignified solemnity with some saintly recreation. The history of the Church furnishes us with many examples. It is to this, without doubt, that one must account for the origin of the pious and modest recreations which our ancestors made on the Day of Resurrection, to the concerts which were chanted in counterpoint, the sequences of the celebration followed later by pastimes such as round dances and games of tennis and ball." This theory of Boutillier in no way conflicts with the theory that the ball games also sprang from pagan customs.

But within the monasteries and the churches the games played quickly developed into a form of tennis to which religious meaning was still attached. By the year 1287, at least within church walls, the rough and tumble ball games had become more refined, and the qualms of the earlier clerics seem to have been temporarily overcome in certain churches: the game of tennis was officially recognized. "On Easter Day, after dinner," it is reported, "the Canon of St. Cyr, at Nevers, joined with the Bishops in believing that their dignity would not suffer by a little volleying of a tennis ball, and the Bishop, far from condemning after the Lenten penitences this innocent pastime, had written in his book of instructions, in 1287, that amongst other duties, should be the obligation to serve refreshments to those in the choir who had taken part" in the game. In the middle of the next century a later Canon of St. Cyr decreed that the balls used in the games should be supplied by the student-priests, as well as the refreshments to all members of the choir on the day following Easter. It is evident that the game of tennis was well established with the clerics of Nevers by the thirteenth century.

These, and other similar regulations, indicate that although other Easter diversions were enjoyed by the people at large, tennis was by preference the game for the clergy—an understandable situation when it is recalled that the game could be played only within large indoor spaces, such as within the confines of ecclesiastical buildings, where the required walls were available.

The Easter customs lasted a long time among the clergy of Auxerre. The ball with which they played at first was evidently quite large. This resulted from the misguided zeal of the young priests who showed their piety and enthusiasm by vying with one another to produce "bigger and better" balls, but on April 19, 1412, it was decreed that the ball be reduced to a smaller size, not so small that it would take two hands to stop it, and that it be offered "with the customary solemnities" and played according to custom. Again, we must remember, racquets were not in use, but the ball played with the hand.

In the year 1471 the Auxerrean custom received a check, when Gérard Royer, a celebrated Parisian theologian was appointed Canon of St. Cyr. On Easter Day, when a large number of the nobility, leading citizens and clergy had assembled to witness the traditional ceremonies, Royer failed to produce the ball. He quoted Beleth and Durandus to support his opposition to the custom. Considerable commotion resulted, and much protest made. Finally the ball which had been used on the previous year was found, and "when the murmurings had ceased," Royer was prevailed upon to present the ball "with doctoral dignity" to the Dean, and the game proceeded. The ceremony existed until 1531, when another Canon again objected. An appeal was made to Francis I, but the matter was not settled. In 1535 further objection was made, and in 1538 an ecclesiastical court decreed that the ceremony should cease.

At the Chapter of Sainte Croix at Orleans, in 1428, there existed another of these "ancient customs," the *redevance des raquettes*, which called for the payment of an annual obligation of racquets and balls. From the Bishop was due to the Chapter a ceremonial repast consisting of a white pigeon and pastries, while the Chapter had to render in return racquets, with which the Bishop played tennis, a custom "well established in the middle ages." Each Easter Day, after the sermon, the Bishop proceeded to his Palace, where he found the Canon of Sainte Croix, who offered him a pair of racquets and some tennis balls. "And so in this manner all in common were obliged not only to participate in the more important acts of worship . . . but also those for relaxation and pleasure."

"This vestige of religious symbols," as Bimbenet calls them, became the subject of litigation at Orleans as they had at Auxerre. The Bishop of Orleans failed to provide the ceremonial repast, whereupon the Chapter brought suit before the Provost of Orleans in order to establish the right, "For sad to relate, these naive ceremonies which harmonized so well with religious sentiment, ceased to be practiced in that spirit. They lost their primitive character to become a matter of contention, and had sunk to the level of a law suit, even as one might demand the execution of a civil contract." Bimbenet expresses the opinion that this legal action "demonstrated clearly that they had lost view of the symbolic character of the custom, for inasmuch as the ceremony of the mystery of the Pentecost had not taken place, of what use was the pigeon?" The judge upheld the complainants, and affirmed their possession of the right as an hereditary obligation, and ordered the restoration of the custom.

A hundred years later, in 1525, another lawsuit involved the obligation of the exchange of racquets. A Bishop, accompanied by the usual crowd of notables, proceeded to the rear of the Church in the traditional manner, but instead of a pair of racquets, the representative of the Chapter offered the cheap substitute of a pair of small batons with which to strike the tennis balls. The Bishop refused the substitute, claimed his right to the racquets, and was later upheld in court.

L'Abbé Cochard has collected many details relating to ecclesiastical tennis. "That the ecclesiastics, bishops, canons and priests exercised at tennis nothing is more certain," he says. "This profane custom was particularly practiced at the Churches of Meaux, Auxerre and Troyes. Since these three Churches were under the jurisdiction of the Archbishop of Sens, one can infer that a similar usage might be found in the metropolitan Chapter, and in that of Orleans." At St. Brieuc the *Acts* of the Chapter record in 1480 "an ancient custom . . . on Easter Day, immediately after the completion of the services, of giving five tennis balls to the Bishop, and three to each of the Canons, and racquets with which to strike them."

L'Abbé Cochard, referring to the above customs, states that "this singular rite was found in many French Churches," and relates how, when interest in the game of tennis increased to such a point that the worthy clerics devoted more attention to it than was deemed advisable, "in order to safeguard ecclesiastical dignity, and to prevent scandal, this tolerance was placed under canonical restriction."

Many of the Councils of Sens held between 1460 and 1485, whose decrees had the force of law in the Diocese of Orleans, forbade "priests and all others in sacred orders from playing tennis without shame, in their undershirts, or not decently dressed." In the Douce Manuscripts at the Bodleian Library is an early sixteenth century illuminated missal which, on the Calendar for November, pictures one of these "scandalous" games, where two clerics play at tennis in a cloister, one of whom has laid aside his religious garb, disclosing his undershirt underneath.

In 1525 Jean de Longueville, who previously had protested against the custom of the presentation of the Easter racquets and balls, confirmed the decisions of the Councils of Sens, and forbade his priests "to play publicly and frequently, above all with the laity." Finally in 1640 Nicolas de Nets promulgated the following article: "It is forbidden to all *curés, beneficiaries, prêtres et autres ecclesiastiques* in our diocese to frequent the public tennis games, on pain of penalty, for the first offense, and of prison if the offense is repeated." Similar regulations were issued in 1642, 1647, 1656 and 1664.

"One might judge," says Cochard, "from these canonical decrees that it was not permissible for the priests of the Church at Orleans to frequent the *public* tennis courts to play tennis with laymen, and it may be concluded that our Canons of Sainte Croix had in their cloisters a tennis court, where they could go but seldom. It was the *Salle du Prétoire de l'Officialité*."

And so the ancient ceremonies of the ball gradually lost their religious significance, their very observance sometimes a matter of legal enforcement, while the interest in the *game* increased until it became necessary to dampen the enthusiasm of the young ecclesiastics for what had become their most popular pastime.

One more instance of the association of tennis with the Church, though non-liturgical, is to be found at Marolles, near Liseaux, where it flourished under the name of *jeu de bonde*. In the later years of the fourteenth century the young people playing this game "made the ball reverberate upon the sloping roof under the *vocable* of St. Martin." This game was also played at Haudivilliers in Beauvais towards the middle of the sixteenth century at the Chapel of Étreham, in the environs of Bayeaux. At Blaincourt in Peronne tennis was played by married men against single men.

Mention has been made of the fact that the shape of a modern court tennis court (not *lawn* tennis) resembles closely that of a monastery cloister. That this is no accident, and indeed bears mute testimony as to the origin of the game is obvious. "We are not surprised," says one authority, "that Julian Marshall (the great historian of tennis) has taken no note of the tradition which almost proves its own truth, that the tennis-court, like the Eton fives-court, was the result of an accident of ground, and is, in fact, the copy of a monastery courtyard turned by the monks to the purpose of an improvised game. The two sides of the cloisters, the sloping roof, the 'tambour' (a buttress projecting from the wall), the 'grille,' with its very name, as the window where friends may be seen; and the tradition, say what we will, is very strong evidence. Be this as it may, the game was first a French one."

55

A modern authority on tennis, Albert de Luze, favors the theory of the monastic origin. "Some authors," he says, "struck by the quasi-monasterial aspect of the tennis courts, have attributed these characteristics to ecclesiastics. This opinion appears to us to be very plausible."

A perfect analogy of the influence of the original site of a game, also of ecclesiastical association, is the game of Eton fives, which may be considered as a complicated variation of handball, played in a court of peculiar, yet definite shape. Eton fives had its origin "amid the mossy drainpipes of an ecclesiastical atmosphere. . . . Under a lenient ecclesiastical wing it has taken its root and developed to its present state. For many centuries the pastime of a few small boys, unofficial and unnoticed by the historian, it remains today a game for the few." The court was the Chapel steps at Eton. "Jutting out from the north wall of the Chapel is the main entrance. From it descends a flight of steps running from east to west, and having a low buttress near the lower end, to serve as a hand rail. The pavement at the bottom of these steps formed the back, or outer court. The small buttress formed the 'Pepper Box.' The upper court consisted of three walls. . . . Finally, the 'Dead Man's Hole' is nothing more or less than one of the drains. In Eton fives, as in real tennis, it is the accidents of the court which provide the true greatness of the game, and its undoubted superiority over all games in which no form of natural hazard exists."

Cumulative evidence shows the ecclesiastical development of the game of tennis, following the introduction of the ball into the ritual of the Church. The early association of the ball with various forms of two-sided contests, as well as the natural inclination to throw or knock it about, undoubtedly proved an incentive to the younger monks, and provided an idea on which to work. The cloister and the courtyard were the natural, if not the only, places for them to play. Slowly the idea of a pastime developed, and as the recreative interest increased the ritualistic elements diminished, until at last an entirely secularized game emerged and the ritual disappeared.

Courtiers playing tennis, France, 1536.

The game passed into secular life, from monastery court-yard and episcopal palace to the castles of the nobility, and finally to the palaces of kings, where special courts were built. The earliest court on record was built at Poitiers in 1230, by Pierre Garnier. By 1292 thirteen professional tennis "masters" appear on the tax list of the City of Paris, and by 1400 the game had so far progressed in France that a Guild of Tennis Masters controlled both the play and the manufacture of racquets and balls. It is not known when or by whom tennis was introduced into England, but it was well established there by the end of the fourteenth century. Some form of the game was played in Scotland during the reign of Alexander III between 1249 and 1285.

By the year 1600 tennis had reached its greatest popularity in France, where the adaptation of the many courts for theatrical purposes aided the rapid development of the theatre. By the time of Shakespeare tennis was the popular game of the common people. Unfortunately, because of its association with gambling and the less desirable "sports" of society who frequented the courts for no good purpose, it waned, until by the beginning of the nineteenth century it had almost disappeared. Today tennis is played in the private courts of a few wealthy men in England and America, and a few select sporting clubs in the United States, England and France. It is a splendid game, ideal for exercise for young and old, but unfortunately restricted in use because of its excessive cost. The game of *longue paume,* or long tennis, a form of the game played in its early days out of doors, is still played in a few places in France.

9. Tennis in English Literature

THE pastimes of a nation are mirrored in its literature. As one sport gives way to another in popular favor, writers of the times record the changing customs. Baseball has found its place in American literature; the modern Englishman writes of foxhunting, and of course the literature of cricket is enormous. But before the year 1700 the one outstanding game reflected in the casual figure of speech of the poet, delineated as accomplishments of the characters in the pages of the dramatist, or considered in the preachments of the moralist, was the ancient game of tennis. The game must have been deeply rooted in the life of the English nation to have gained such a prominent place in its literature.

By the time of the Tudors tennis, which earlier had crossed from France, was well established as the game of the courtier and the gentleman. Indeed its popularity spread so rapidly amongst the common people also, that Estienne Perlin, in his *Description of England and Scotland*, 1558, could write: "Here you may commonly see artisans, such as hatters and joiners, playing at tennis for a crown, which is not commonly seen elsewhere, particularly on a working day."

But tennis fell into bad repute. The courts became the favorite resorts of gamblers and all sorts of persons of doubtful character, until by the end of the seventeenth century, the game was almost stifled out of existence by the blanket of obloquy which enfolded it. Yet, well into the eighteenth century the fashionable young men, the "fops," were still being satirized in the contemporary comedies of manners for their attendance at the courts, not for exercise or for the acquiring of skill at the game, but merely to be in keeping with the fashionable follies of their day.

Sidelights of tennis illuminate historical incidents, adding perhaps not so much of historical value, but humanizing the characters, making them a little more real to the modern student. For example, Henry Howard, Earl of Surrey, as a youth spent many happy hours in Windsor Castle. Later, when he had the misfortune to be imprisoned there, he passed the slow hours in writing his *Songes and Sonnettes* (1557), in which "he recounteth his pleasures there passed," one of which was the "palme-play" as tennis was then called:

> *So cruel prison how could betide, alas,*
> *As proud Windsor, where I in lust and joy,*
> *With a Kinge's son, my childish years did pass,*
> *In greater feast than Priam's son of Troy,*
> *Where each sweet place returns a taste full sour.*
>
> *The palme-play, where, despoiled for the game,*
> *With dazed eyes oft we by gleams of love*
> *Have miss'd the ball, and got sight of our dame,*
> *To bait her eyes, which kept the leads above.*

Edmund Spenser in the *Faerie Queen* uses a tennis figure of speech in expressing ideas on the defense of Ulster, but the incident of Henry V and the Dauphin's gift of tennis balls,

Women playing a game of ball, France, 1344.

La soule played by ecclesiastics in France, 1344.

Stoolball, as played in France, 1344.

Tennis played in a cloister, 1497.

Tennis played in cloister, early 16th century.

Jeu de la Crosse, France, 18th Century.

told by Shakespeare, is known to every schoolboy. Its fascination for the historian is evident, for it is told in *The Brut*, Froissart, Hall and Higden, and dramatized both by Michael Drayton and the anonymous *Famous Victories of Henry V.* Elias Ashmole naively refers to the incident in his discussion of the legendary origin of the Order of the Garter, which credits the chivalrous King Edward III with stooping to pick up the garter of Joan, Countess of Salisbury. He objected to the legend because "It might be expected that some historian among the French (who were so forward as to jeer at our King Henry the Fifth's design for invading them, with a return of tennis balls) would not have forborn to register somewhere or other, a scoff at the Ladies Garter." The inimitable diarist Pepys describes a game played by Charles II, and the custom the King "usually hath of weighing himself before and after the play, to see how much he loses in weight by playing: and this day he lost 4½ lbs." Evidently His Majesty played a vigorous game.

Curiously enough, in spite of the popularity of tennis in England for centuries, there was no handbook of the game until modern times. The Italian Scaino in 1555, and the French Forbet in 1592 give the early rules, but our knowledge of the game in England depends on incidental allusions in unexpected places. One of the most informative of these is an Italian-English conversation book, written by John Florio, a tutor in the Royal household. A conversation book, perhaps, should not be classed as "literature," yet there is a certain style and vividness about *Second Frutes* that compels attention, and as an account of the manners and customs of the time, it is invaluable. A game of tennis is described, and the "faire white balls" with which it is played. The players placed

61

"the stake money under the line," counted by fifteens, and after the game paid for "three dozen and a halfe" balls.

John Stowe's *Survay of London* (1603) states that "the ball is used by noblemen and gentlemen in tennis courts," implying that the game was not one enjoyed by ordinary people, a surprising contrast to the evidence of Estienne Perlin scarcely fifty years earlier. There can be no doubt, however, that throughout the seventeenth century the gentlemen of the court, and the well-to-do played the game and delighted in it. In the 1653 edition of Walton's *Compleat Angler* there appeared *The Angler's Song*, said to have been written by William Basse. It begins:

> As inward love breeds outward talk,
> The hound some praise, and some the hawk:
> Some better pleased with private sport
> Use tennis, some a mistress sport.
> > But these delights I neither wish,
> > Nor envy, while I freely fish.

And that spendthrift of the Restoration, Phil Porter, in his *Wit and Drollery*, laments his enforced absence from the courts:

> Farewell my dearest Piccadilly,
> Notorious for great Dinners,
> Oh what a tennis court was there!
> Alas! Too good for Sinners.

Since tennis was first played it has been the custom to play with solid balls. Many materials were used to stuff the leather casings, wool being the most frequently used. Measures occasionally had to be taken to prevent the ancient ball makers from using sawdust and such like materials, some of which were injurious to the hands. It seems to have been the general practice during the sixteenth and seventeenth centuries, at least in England, to use human hair. The obvious sources of supply were the barbers' shops of the town, and the destination of the clippings of the beards and hair of the barbers' clients was common knowledge. Thus we find in the *Prognostication* of the satirist Thomas Nashe (1591), the dire prophecy that "whereas the Eclipse falleth out at three of the clocke in the afternoone, it forsheweth that many shall go soberer into Tavernes than shall come out . . . that some shall have so sore a sweating, that they may sell their haire by the pound to stuff tennice balles."

In Shakespeare's *Much Ado About Nothing* Claudio, in response to Don Pedro's playful remark about Benedick, "Hath any man seen him at the Barber's?" replies, "No, but the barber's man hath been seen with him, and the old ornament of his cheek hath already stuffed tennis-balls."

The staunch loyalty of Eyre in Thomas Dekker's *The Shoemaker's Holiday* (1600) finds an unusual form of expression:

> KING: Tell me in faith, mad Eyre, how old thou art?
> EYRE: My Liege, a very boy, a stripling, a yonker, you see not a white haire on my head, nor a gray in this beard, every haire, I assure thy Majesty that sticks in this beard, Sim Eyre valews at the King of Babilon's ransome, Tamar Cham's beard was a rubbing brush to't, yet I'le shave it off, and stuffe tennis balls with it to please my bully King.

There is a stirring example of patriotism! Sir Oliver Small-Shanks in the anonymous drama *Ram Alley* (1611) was not in such a happy frame of mind under the prospective loss of his beard when Puff threatened him: "If you come there, Thy beard shall serve to stuff those balls by which I get me heat at tennis."

In the minds of the people of England during the Tudor and Stuart periods, it was evidently considered "French," and therefore foppish to play tennis, and the satirists of the day were quick to poke fun at the addicts of the game. If the word of Sir R. A. Dallington can be taken, in his *Method for Travell* (1598), it is no wonder that the game was considered to be "French," for it enjoyed an amazing popularity across the Channel. "As for the exercise of tennis," he says, "it is here more used than in all Christendome besides . . . yee cannot find that little burgade or towne in France, that hath not one or more (courts). . . . Me thinks it is also strange how apt they be here to play well, that ye would thinke they were borne with Rackets in their hands. . . . There be more Tennis Players in France than aledrinkers, or maltwormers (as they call them) with us."

Note the derision in Mercury's description of Hedon in Ben Jonson's *Cynthia's Revels:* "He courts ladies with how many great horse he hath rid that morning, or how oft he hath done the whole, or half the pommado (that is, to mount his horse without the aid of stirrups) in the seven-night before: and sometimes ventures so far upon the virtue of his pomander that he dares to tell 'em how many shirts he has sweat at tennis that week, but wisely conceals so many dozen of balls he is on the score." Tennis was undoubtedly a requisite of the elegant gentleman.

Thomas Dekker, in his *Guls Horne-booke* (1609) speaks in the same strain, but with a delicate scorn of the French added: "If you be a courtier . . . discourse how often this lady hath sent her coach for you: how often you have sweat in the tennis court with that great lord: for indeede, the sweating in France (I meane the Society of Tennis) is a great argument of most deere affection, even between noble men and pesants." Again, in John Webster's *Duchess of Malfi* (1612), Delio speaks in the same temper:

> *Now sir, your promise, what's that Cardinal?*
> *I mean his temper? they say he's a brave fellow,*
> *Will play his five thousand crowns at tennis, dance,*
> *Court ladies, and one that hath fought single combats.*

In 1535 Henry VIII had forbidden any to keep houses for "tenys or other unlawful games," and in Shakespeare's *Henry VIII* Sir Thomas Lovell looks with approval on the restrictions upon "our travell'd gallants," and the baneful influence of the French upon them:

> *They must either*
> *(For so run the conditions) leave these remnants*
> *Of fool, and feather, that they got in France,*
> *With all their honourable points of ignorance*
> *Pertaining thereunto . . .*
> *renouncing clean*
> *The faith they have in tennis and tall stockings,*
> *Short blistered breeches, and those types of travel,*
> *And understand again like honest men.*

Nor does Beaumont and Fletcher's *Scornful Ladie* look with favor upon a trip to France by a lover: "And all these (almost invisible labours) performed for your Mistress, to be in danger to forsake her, and to put on new allegiance to some *French* Lady, who is content to change a language with your laughter, and after your whole year spent in tennis and broken speech, to stand the hazard of being laught at, at your return."

Naturally the university men would not be slow to adopt as their own the French-tennis manners of the period, in fact it became almost a necessity to acquire them. J. Earle, a Fellow of Merton, Oxford, in his *Micro-Cosmographie* (1628), in describing "a mere young Gentleman of the Universitie," specifies that "the two markes of his Senioritie, is the bare Velvet of his Gowne, and his proficiencie at Tennis, where, when he can once play a Set, he is a Fresh-man no more."

We have seen how some of the gallants of the day boasted of the number of sweat-shirts they used at tennis. It was the duty of the tennis-court keeper to care for the shirts and other wearing apparel of the game used by his patrons. For instance, Prince Henry, in Shakespeare's *Second Part of King Henry the Fourth* tells Poins indignantly: "What a disgrace . . . to bear the inventory of thy shirts; as, one for superfluity, and the other for use! but that the tennis-court-keeper knows better than I, for it is a low ebb of linen with thee when thou keepest not racket there."

In the *Play of Stucley* (1605), amongst the many claims made on Stucley when he comes into a fortune is one by a tennis-court-keeper appropriately named Hazard:

> CURTIS: There's a knave, what's his legacy?
> STUCLEY: For tennis balls when the French Ambassador was here, thirteen pound. Was it so much?
> HAZARD: Just so much, with the fouling of fair linen when you were hot.
> CURTIS: Fair linen! Hoy day! Your fair linen wipes him of a good deal of money.
> STUCLEY: George Hazard, I take it that's your name?
> HAZARD: My name it is so, Sir.
> CURTIS: George, you have hit the hazard.
> *(Gives him the money.)*

Brachiano, however, in John Webster's *The White Devil* (1612), changed his linen occasionally at his lady's house, and thereby got into trouble:

FRANCISCO DE MEDICI: You know Vittoria?
BRACHIANO: Yes.
FRANCISCO DE MEDICI: You shift your shirt there
when you retire from tennis?
BRACHIANO: Happily. (i.e., Perhaps.)

And in *The Honest Man's Fortune* of Beaumont and Fletcher
the tennis shirt comes aptly to the tongue of Longueville:

AMIENS: Let it suffice I leave
My honour to your guard, and in that prove
You hold the first place in my heart and love.
LONGUEVILLE: The first place in a lord's affection!
very good: and how long doth that last? perhaps the
changing of some three shirts in the tennis court.

Gambling became associated with tennis quite early in its
history, and wherever it was played. The rules of the game
scarcely exceeded in importance the tables of odds to be laid
as the game progressed. As might be expected, the literature
of the game contains many allusions to this unfortunate com-
bination. One of the earliest characters addicted to the double
pastime was the Scotch parson in Sir David Lindsay's *Ane
Satyre* (1535), who boasted:

Thocht I preich not, I can play at the caiche (tennis).
I wait thair is nocht ane amang you all,
Mair ferilie can play at the futball:
And for the carts, the tabels, and the dyse,
Aboue all persouns I may beir the pryse.

A veritable sporting parson! Here we see the familiar association of tennis not only with gambling in the courts, but with
other forms, such as card playing and dice. Nor do we find
that contemporary writers approved of the association: practically unanimously they condemned it. The speech of Per-
verse doctrine in the morality play *New Custom* (1573), is
decidedly derisive:

Give them that which is meete for them, a racket and a ball,
Or some other trifle, to busy their heads withal.

For thoroughgoing denunciation of tennis, one naturally looks to the puritanically minded writers, such as Richard Rice, who in his *Invective against the Vices taken for Vertue* (1579), leaves no doubt in the reader's mind as to his adverse opinion of the game: "Will ye see what goodnesse ensueth of your honest termed pastimes: firste, where doe children piteously crye out for meate and drinke and cannot get it? forsoothe where their father is given to bowlyng, dicyng or cardyng, tennis plaiyng, scailyng and suche like. Where doe servauntes lacke woorke, and stand whirlyng their knife about the stretes and walles, to occupie the whole halfe daie in vain language? Where their masters be addicte to . . . tennisplaiyng and such like. . . . Honeste recreations are meete for honeste men, but cardyng . . . tennis plaiyng are not honest recreations: Ergo they are not meete for honeste men." It is not surprising to find that Rice included in his "Vices" the seemingly innocent game of chess.

In the *Anatomy of the Abuses of England* (1583), the pamphleteer Philip Stubbes echoes the attack of Rice, if not surpasses it in virulence: The landlords "inhance the rents" and spend their ill-gotten gains in "dicing, carding, bowling, tennise plaeing . . . and other the like prophane exercises. . . . As for tennise, and such like, thei are all *furta officiosa*, a certain kind of smooth deceitfull, and sleightie thefte, whereby many a one is spoiled of all that ever he hath." Even in the mind of Shakespeare there evidently existed this same association of the tennis courts with scoundrels of low type, for does not Polonius, coaching Reynaldo to spy upon Laertes while in Paris, suggest a sample conversation with a stranger:

Or then, or then, with such, or such, and, as you say,
There was he gaming, there o'ertook in's rouse,
There falling out at tennis.

The ready wit of Anamnestes in the anonymous *Lingua* (1607), saves him from a somewhat critical situation:

> ANAM: In truth, sir, I was here before, and missing you, went back into the city, sought you in every ale-house, tavern dicing house, tennis-court, stews, and such like places, likely to find your worship in.
> MEMORIA: Ha, villain, am I a man likely to be found in such places, ha?
> ANAM: No, no, sir, but I was told by my lady Lingua's page that your worship was seeking me, therefor I enquired for you in those places where I knew you would ask for me, an' it please your worship.

And so on. There are many such incidents recorded. But by the year 1699, if we can believe *The Country Gentleman's Vade-Mecum,* the moral tone of the tennis courts had fallen to a very low ebb. This little book states that: "There are but few Matches made, but there was either a bribed Marker, or some Gentleman that had first lost his Estate, and then his Honour, and so was forc'd to comply with the Sharpings and Tricks of the Town, to get his bread; or some Scoundrel that never had an Estate or Honour either, but had acquired the game by a diligent attendance upon the courts . . . and there was hardly a Set play'd but there was some sort of Falshood and Deceit practic'd."

10. Stoolball

THE game of stoolball has never rivalled cricket or football in popularity, but it has been played by small groups, chiefly in country places, for over six hundred years. It is of great interest because it has long been considered to be an ancestor of cricket. It is also a direct forbear of America's national pastime, baseball. In 1916 an attempt was made to revive the old game, although in revised form, using a small square target raised on a stump instead of a stool. It became so popular that a Stoolball Association was formed in 1927 which now has over 3000 clubs.

Four characteristics of the old game of stoolball are very evident: first, the constant association of the game with the Church, and the churchyard as the place where it was usually played; second, its association with the Easter season; third, it was always played by young men and maidens, and fourth, the use of flavored cakes, usually tansy, as prizes.

It has been claimed that ball play was introduced into England by St. Cuthbert, who was said to have played ball with children, but St. Bede made no mention of St. Cuthbert's prowess with the ball when he wrote his life. It is remarkable that so many of the earlier instances of ball play in England have something to do with Easter. For example, a thirteenth century account of London school-boy customs by Fitz-stephen relates that "annually upon Shrove Tuesday they go into the fields immediately after dinner, and play at the celebrated game of ball, every party of boys carrying their own ball." Just what kind of ball they played is not known, but it was a well established Easter custom, with the ball bearing a major part in the proceedings.

In 1553, at the Easter Sessions of a court at Maldon, in Surrey, five men were indicted for playing stoolball on Sunday, April 14th. In 1623, again at Maldon, some young men were haled before the Easter Session for playing the game.

And the element of romance—it was definitely a period of merrymaking of particular concern to young men and maidens, a time for courting *par excellence*. There can be no doubt that this characteristic of the Easter stoolball festivities has a direct association with the ancient pagan rites, with connotations of human fertility and child-bearing. This is well shown in D'Urfey's *Pills to purge melancholy*, a collection of rather *risqué* poems, including one from a play *Don Quixote*, acted at Dorset Green in 1694. The first verse reads:

> *Down in the vale on a Summer's day,*
> *All the lads and lasses went to be merry,*
> *A match for kisses at Stoolball to play,*
> *And for cakes and ale, and sider and perry.*
> *Chorus: Come all, great small,*
> *Short tall, away to Stoolball.*

A more sedate specimen is called:

> Stool-Ball, or the Easter Diversion.
> *When now the time for Penance past,*
> *The self denying days of fast,*

71

Nature with vigor blooms anew,
And shows a more enlivening view.
Cold wintry seasons far retir'd
And all with vernal warmth inspir'd.
The beauteous maids and willing swains
In scenes of frolic crowd the plains;
And to the Spring their honours pay,
In rites of customary play . . .

Describe, my Muse, the annual play
In which they waste the festal day . . .
Obsequious youths their pleasure wait,
Each proud to chuse a lovely mate.
At upper end is fixed the stool,
In fam'd heroick games the goal;
Not sacred tripod as of old,
But quadruped of modern mold . . .

Two genial parts the match divide,
Proportion just on either side . . .

See at the goal Pulcheria stand
And grasp the board with snowy hand!
She drives the ball with artful force
Guiding through hostile ranks its course . . .

Where does the shame or crime appear
Of harmless romping once a year?

Another curious association of the Easter ball game in England was the custom of awarding the winner a "tansy" cake, that is, a small cake flavored with tansy, a bitter herb. Or, as in some places, a "tansy" was the name of the village merrymaking held on Shrove Tuesday, for which the tansy cakes were specially prepared. This recalls the old customs in the Churches of France during the middle ages, when ceremonial feasts were part of the Easter ceremonies. A more ancient origin, but one in direct line, which has been suggested, is that the tansy cakes originated from the Jewish custom of eating bitter herbs at the time of the Passover, a theory which takes us back to Biblical times, and is most plausible.

Another Easter ball custom at Newcastle, in the north of England, was a little more formal than the earlier London ways. "Anciently," the Mayor, Aldermen and Sheriffs accompanied by a large number of the leading citizens of the city, each Whitsuntide would proceed in a formal procession to a square in the center of the city, carrying all their symbols of office: the mace, the sword and the cap of maintenance. When they reached the square, the young people would play games of ball. As recently as 1810 Strutt recorded that young people still continued to assemble there at Whitsuntide and play at "handball."

That stoolball was merely a local adaptation of the ancient pagan rites there can be no doubt, and many writers have suspected it. An English clergyman, Henry Bourne, writing in 1725, tackled the problem of the origin of the curious Easter ball games. Why the ball games were so popular at the Easter season instead of other games puzzled him. But he did come to the conclusion, although without presenting evidence, that "it will be readily granted that the twelfth century Easter ball ceremonies in the Churches of France, and decried by some of the theologians of the time, were the origin of our present recreations and diversions on Easter Holy Days, and in particular the playing of ball for a tanzy cake, which at this season is generally practiced; and I would hope practiced with harmlessness and innocence. For when the common devotions of the day are over, there is nothing sinful in lawful recreation."

The reverend gentleman made a good guess. The "games" as played in the French churches were indeed the forbears of the English Easter games of the sixteenth, seventeenth and eighteenth centuries, but they went much further back than that to the ancient pagan festivals, such as the *Saturnalia*, when license and abandon were the order of the day. Their real nature is more than suggested in *Pasquil's Palinodia*, written in 1634, which describes Shrove Tuesday customs in England. We quote in part:

> It was the day of all dayes in the yeare
> That unto Bacchus hath its dedication,
> When mad-brained Prentices, that no men fear,
> O'erthrow the dens of bawdy recreation . . .
> It was the day when Pullen go to block,
> And every spit is fill'd with belly timber,
> When cocks are cudgelled down with many a knock,
> And hens are thrashed to make them short and tender,
> When Country Wenches play with Stoole and Ball,
> And run at barley-breake untill they fall!

Stoolball was played in England probably as early as 1330, when William Pagula, Vicar of Winkfield, near Windsor, wrote in Latin a poem of instructions to parish priests, advising them to forbid the playing of all games of ball in church-yards:

> Bat and bares and suche play
> Out of chyrche-yorde put away.

Undoubtedly the festivals of the Easter ball in England were beginning to lose some of their religious significance, as it had been lost in France, and the clergy were making efforts to break away from the association of the ball with the Church. In 1450 John Myrc, a canon at Lilleshall Monastery, translated the poem into English, a commentary on the latinity of the clergy of the day. On the margin of the Myrc manuscript, however (and it may be seen at the Bodleian Library in

Oxford), some unknown scribe, a contemporary of Myrc, added a note explaining that the games to which Pagula alluded were bowling, tennis, handball, football and stoolball.

Stoolball was very simple at first, befitting a game in which young men and women played together. A three-legged stool was upended. A batter stood before the stool either bare handed, or with some form of a bat. A player was "out" if a ball hit the stool, or the ball was caught after being struck, and another player took his place at the stool. The winner was the player who scored the greatest number of hits. This, however, is an eighteenth-century description. Exactly how they played earlier cannot be clearly ascertained.

One author claims that the game of Bittle-Battle, mentioned in the *Domesday Book*, the famous survey of England made by command of William the Conqueror, and finished in 1086, was a form of stoolball. It might have been, for a "bittle" or "beetle" is a stick with some kind of a head, with which balls could have been struck. Further, this suggests that the Easter ball games were introduced into England by William the Conqueror's men. But of course this is highly conjectural.

There was nothing to prevent the playing of stoolball at other times than Easter, and although the Easter customs persisted, the game, naturally popular with young people, particularly those amorously inclined to "co-ed" pastimes, was played occasionally throughout the year. Nevertheless the Easter stoolball in many country places in England was the time above all times for love making, which undoubtedly led to a permanent pairing of many ball-playing couples.

It so happens that stoolball was the first ball game recorded as being played in the American colonies by the Pilgrims. Late in the year 1621 the good ship *Fortune* brought to Plymouth Colony thirty-five newcomers, most of whom were "lusty yonge men, and many of them wilde enough." When Christmas Day arrived, the Pilgrims according to their custom, for the need was great, went to work, expecting the new arrivals to do the same. But the young men objected on the ground that it was against their conscience to work on Christmas Day. Governor Bradford, being a reasonable man, accepted their point of view and excused them from work, saying that he "would spare them till they were better informed." And so Bradford and the old timers went off to work, leaving the newcomers behind.

When the Governor and his fellow workers came home at noon for their mid-day meal, however, he was astonished to find the conscientious young men playing a hot game of stool-ball! That was too much for the Governor, and quickly got his dander up. Going up to them, he grabbed "the implements" away from them. It was against *his* conscience that some should work while others played, he protested, and back to work the young men went.

Like all simple games, as players become more expert, stoolball became more complicated, various localities experimented with little refinements, but in spite of the introduction of later combinations, the older forms of the game continued to be played. The first step to "improve" stoolball, played with one upturned stool, with its three legs sticking up into the air, was to add one more stool. Now, in olden days, stools were also called "crickets," and obviously a pitch with two three-legged stools, one at each end with legs in air, is a form of primitive cricket, the popular English game of today. Undoubtedly the newer form was not invented overnight. Rather, over a long period, the new game gradually took form, a process common to other ball games. It is extremely difficult from the data available in the fourteenth and fifteenth centuries to differentiate between the many games played with club and ball.

As long ago as 1815 Peter Roberts, an antiquarian, who was studying the ball games of the Easter season noted the similarity between stoolball and cricket. "Another species of this game called stool-ball," we read, "resembling cricket, except that no bats are used, and that a stool is a substitute for the wicket, was in my memory, also a favorite game on Holy Days, but is now, like many other rural games, I believe, seldom if ever played. These amusements generally began on Easter Eve, and were resumed after Easter Day."

The next step to a two-wicket, or two-base game is to add one, and then more bases, and in time this was done: there is plenty of evidence to prove it. For instance, *The Little Pretty Pocket Book*, a small gilt-paper bound juvenile published first in 1744, but of which the 1767 edition is the earliest *extant*, has a page devoted to stoolball. At the top of the page is a large three-legged stool. Then appears an illustration captioned: "Stool-Ball," in which there are three players, the batter standing at a stool, one serving the ball, and a third standing at first base. Next there follows a children's poem:

STOOLBALL

The ball once struck with art and care,
And drove impetuous through the air;
Swift round his course the Gamster flies,
Or his stool's taken by surprise.
   Rule of Life.
Bestow your alms whene'er you see
An object of necessity.

This clearly implies a number of stools, with a player at each stool who may be put out if the ball is thrown in his direction, that is, whenever the man who has the ball sees "an object of necessity."

Strutt clearly describes a game played with several stools: "Again in other parts of the country a certain number of stools are set up in circular form, and at a distance from each other. Everyone of them is occupied by a player. When the ball is struck, which is done as before with the hand, they are everyone of them obliged to alter his situation, running in succession from stool to stool. If he who threw the ball can regain it in time to strike any one of the players, before he reaches the stool to which he is running, he takes his place." By this time, we have a ball game in which the players run a circuit of bases when the ball is hit by the batter, still called stoolball. The batter is "out" if struck by a ball between bases, obviously a form of "Rounders" and an early form of baseball.

As the number of bases was increased stones or other objects were used to mark them. Occasionally wooden stakes took the place of stones. In the 1744 illustration we find stakes, and in the *Rules* of the "Massachusetts Game" of baseball as played in America in 1858, we find the stipulation that the bases shall be wooden stakes four and one half feet high.

11. Football

FOOTBALL enthusiasts are apt to claim that the annual "celebrated game of ball" of William Fitzstephen, in his *History of London*, about 1175, is the earliest reference to football in England. It is also claimed that football was forbidden by Edward II in 1314. This statute spoke of "the great noise in the city caused by hustling over large balls (*rageries de grosses pelotes*)." Neither of these references can be taken definitely as "football," and it is very doubtful if football were intended. On the contrary the "annual" occurrence of Fitzstephen and the noisy hustling in the streets of the city over large balls might very well describe spring-time ball customs similar in intent and purpose to those we have seen popularized in France before they settled down into English secularized games, of which football was probably the earliest. Later, in 1365, we find *ad pilam . . . pedinam*, which might more accurately be translated "football," prohibited with other games because they interfered with the military preparedness of the time—proficiency in archery. Men were warned not to waste time playing useless games of ball when they should be improving their marksmanship with bow and arrow. Many times later this prohibition was repeated.

But we are not surprised to find many references to football played at the Easter season, or in very close association with Shrove Tuesday, just before Lent. On this day local customs in which a game of football was the main feature, took place in many villages throughout England and Scotland. In some places these customs exist to this day.

Prof. F. P. Magoun, Jr., of Harvard has collected a number of examples of Shrove Tuesday football games. The earliest record quoted by Magoun is the custom at Chester in 1533: "It is ordered, assented and agreed by Henry Gee, Mayor of the City of Chester . . . that the said ʹoccupations of shoemakers, which have always, time out of man's remembrance, given and delivered yearly upon Tuesday, commonly called Shrove Tuesday . . . unto the drapers, before the Mayor of the City, at the Cross upon the Rood Dee, one ball of leather, called a football . . . to play at thence to the Common Hall of the said City."

Shortly after this, at Dorset, the Company of Freemen Marblers of Corfe Castle are recorded as participating in Shrove Tuesday football, the football being provided by "the last married man." Brand notes a late custom of the colliers in the north of England: "It is customary for a party to watch the bridegroom coming out of a Church after the ceremony, in order to demand money for a foot-ball, a claim which admits of no refusal." In Duns, Berwickshire, as late as 1835, a ball game was played between married and single men. At Inversk, Midlothian, we read of Shrove Tuesday football between "married and unmarried women, in which the former are always victors." At Scone, the game on Shrove Tuesday was played between bachelors and married men. In this game, however, no one was allowed to kick the ball. "The object of the married men was to hang it, i.e., put it three times in a small hole in the moor, the dool, or limit, on the one hand; that of the bachelors was to drown it, i.e., to dip it three times into a deep place in the river, the limit of the other."

At Alnwick, in Northumberland, the game was played between married men and unmarried. Magoun records such games in no less than forty-two towns, with interesting local variations, in England and Scotland, some of which are observed to this day. He then goes on to say: "In a few parts of the world, at least, football is indisputably ritualistic, and for aught we know, the first football ever kicked on British soil may have been the head of a defeated chieftain. We cannot, if we would, deny the possibility that one of these same prehistoric footballs symbolized the fertilizing sun, or that the game itself represented a once bitter intertribal contest. Yet, were this demonstrable, it would shed but little light on the origin either of ordinary popular football, or of the Shrove Tuesday game still played in England, and for just this reason: that there would not be one scrap of evidence pointing to a continuity between such a prehistoric heathen past and our games as the first appear on record."

Magoun is commendably cautious: while he does not accept, he does not deny the theory of the ritualistic origin of football. He claims that football is mentioned as a game in the statute of 1314, more than two hundred years before the Shrove Tuesday football of 1533. But the latter reference states that Shrove Tuesday football was old "beyond man's remembrance." The earliest date, 1450, is consistent with the theory that the pagan rites spread throughout southern

Europe with the Moors. Indeed, we may claim that this study produces evidence of the continuity which Prof. Magoun requires, and provides the missing link between the pagan fertility rite of ancient Egypt and Arabia, Christian ritual, and modern games such as football, tennis and other games played with bat and ball.

12. Bridal Ball

IT IS interesting to see how in Germany and in some parts of France, the symbolic ball branched away from the rougher games, and associated themselves with more sentimental bridal customs, known in Germany as *Der Brautball,* or Bridal Ball. Moreover these bridal customs were usually observed at the Easter season, and frequently took place in or near the local Church. Occasionally they involved the singing of rhymed praises to the "green leaf."

In Tangermunde, for example, the women who had been married during the past year asked on the third day of Easter for the bridal ball, which was then, amidst such merrymaking, smashed to pieces amongst the fir trees by the farm laborers and maidservants. Near Schwedel, on Easter Sunday, a song of the bridal ball was sung by young people, who had assembled at the home of a newly married couple. In Camern, near Sandow on the Elbe, similar customs were observed with the singing of the song:

> *Green leaf! Green leaf! Prize above all!*
> *This summer, this summer,*
> *All the girls still live.*

We demand the bridal ball!
And if she does not give the ball
We'll take away her man!

In the Parish of Vieux-Pont, in Normandy, the young husband last married before Palm Sunday, had to throw a ball into which he had previously placed some coins, from the foot of the Cross, over the Church. On the other side of the Church waited an eager crowd of youngsters, who scrambled for the ball and its contents. In other places in Normandy the bride had to throw the ball over the local Church, while the bachelors and married men strove for its possession. Sometimes, as in Arendsee in Altmark, balls of various kinds were distributed to various groups, children, apprentices and former friends of the bride. In Ellichsleben a couple who remained childless throughout the year, threw out to the waiting youths a large ball, studded with pins pointed outwards. It was considered a badge of honor to get and hold this one!

"The bridal ball," says Mannhardt, "must have stood in some close relation to the green leaf, to fresh vegetation. . . . It seems to have been essential to the young married couple. . . . May the whole custom of the bridal ball at Easter have been of ecclesiastical origin, descended from Christian symbolism?" And he answers his own question: "The significance of the rite of the Easter balls is shown by the circumstance that Church polity regarded it as necessary to consecrate and even to Christianize it, while it undoubtedly hoped to give a new interpretation to it by use in the Divine Service, as a symbol of Christ Himself."

13. Hurling. Knappan and Shinty

AS WE have seen, as time elapsed the ancient Easter ball games, spreading from place to place, were adapted to local custom. Each place developed details and variations according to the predilections of the people, or perhaps by mere chance some feature would become engrafted into the traditions of the inhabitants of a particular place. In many forms, but always with the central connotation of the ancient agricultural rites, the ball customs would be carried on as local customs, the original purpose completely forgotten, and unknown to the occasional recorder who notes them. Such a writer as recently as the year 1946 in *The Field* described Cornish hurling as it is today, but with no attempt to interpret its significance.

Such local ball customs are known as hurling in Cornwall and Ireland, knappan in Wales and shinty in Scotland. It should be noted, however, that a modern variety of hurling in Ireland, instead of resembling a game of hockey, as in former days, consists of a competition to hurl, or throw a heavy ball to a given point in the fewest number of throws. Total throws are not counted, but only the net difference between the contestants as the game proceeds. It is possible that this form of the game may have had some influence in the development of golf. But the older forms of the game were all fiercely fought club-and-ball traditional games, usually held in the springtime of the year. Gougaud has demonstrated the close similarity of these games to the older *la soule,* coming by way of Brittany, especially the Armorican Coast, to Cornwall.

J. H. Mathews states that from time immemorial the practice has obtained of "throwing the silver ball" at Saint Ives, in Cornwall, on the feastentide. Similar customs are observed at St. Colomb and St. Blazey on the anniversary of the dedication of the Church. Saint Ives' Feast is governed by Candlemas Day. On the following Monday, the inhabitants assemble on the beach, when a ball, which is left in the custody of the Mayor, is thrown from the Churchyard to the crowd. Sides are formed. A pole is erected on the beach, and each side strives to deposit the ball at the pole as many times as possible. Local tradition says that the contest used to be between the Parishes of Ludgvan, Lelant and Saint Ives.

Carew gives a long description of hurling as it was in 1799: "Hurling taketh his denomination from throwing of the ball. . . . There are 15. 20. or 30. players more or less chosen out on each side . . . Some indifferent person throweth up a ball, the which whosoever can catch, and carry through his adversaries goale hath wonne the game . . . The hurlers are bound by the observation of many laws (one of which was the prohibition of a forward pass) . . . He may not throw it to any of his mates standing nearer the goale than himselfe . . . These hurling matches are mostly used at weddings, where commonly the ghests undertake to encounter all comers . . . (Sometimes parish played against parish) Their goales are (sometimes) three or four miles asunder. (A silver ball was used.) You shall sometimes see 20. or 30. lie tugging together in the water, scrambling and scratching for the ball . . . I cannot well resolve whether I should more commend to the game, for the manhood and exercise, or condemne it for the boysterousnes and harm which it begetteth . . . When the hurling is ended you shall see them retyring home, as from a pitched battaile, with bloody pates, bones broken, and out of ioynt, and such bruises as serve to shorten their lives."

The Welsh game of knappan as described in early records is almost identical with hurling. This connection, as well as a claim to greater antiquity, has been noted by Peter Roberts. Knappan, he says, was "used in ancient tyme among . . . our ancient cozens the Cornish men . . . the selfe same exercise . . . which they call hurling, whereby it seemeth that this exercise is more ancient than formerly observed . . . descended to us Welshmen from our first progenitors, the Trojans." This, in the light of modern research, seems to be a shrewd guess.

Knappan was well established in at least five towns, on different days, but all within the Lenten season. It was a decidedly "rugged" game, calling for great stamina as Roberts testifies: "The two companies, being come together about one or two of the clock in the afternoone, beginneth the play in this sort. After a crye made, both parties draw together into some plaine, all first stripped bare, saving a light paire of breeches, bare headed, bare bodied, bare legges and feete, their cloathes layd together in great heapes . . . for if he leave but his shirt on his backe, in the furie of the

game it is most commonly torne to pieces . . . There is a
round bowle prepared of a reasonable quantitie (size), soe
as a man may hold it in his hand, and noe more . . . boyled
in tallowe to make it slippery . . . This bowle is called
knappan, and is by one of the company hurled bolt upright
to the ayere, and at the falle, he that catcheth it hurleth it
towards the countey he playeth for, (for gole or appointed
place there is none, neither needeth any) for the play is not
given over until the knappan be so far carried that there is
no hope to returne it backe that night . . . The knappan
being cast forth you shall see the same tossed backwarde and
forwarde, by hurling throwes in straunge sorte; for in three
or four throwes, you shall see the whole body of the game
removed half a mile or more, and in this sort it is a strange
sight to see 1000 or 1500 naked men to come neere together
in a cluster followinge the knappan . . . There are, besides
the corps or mayne body of the play, certaine scoutes or forerunners, whose charge is alwaies to keepe before the knappan
which way soever it passes; these alwaies be of the adverse
partie, between the other partie and home, least by surrep-
tion the knappan should be snatched by a borderer of the
game, and so carried away by foote or by horse . . . In this
sorte you shall in an open field see 2000 naked people follow
the bowle backwarde and forwarde, East, West, South and
North, so that a straunger that casuallie should see such a
multitude soe ranging naked, would think them distracted
. . . In the furie of the chase they respect neither hedge,
ditch, pale or walle, hille, dale, bushes, river or rocke, or any
other passable impediment . . . The horsemen have mon-
strous codgells . . . as big as the party is able to weld, and

he that thinketh himself well horsed maketh means to his friends of the footmen to have the knappan delivered to him, which being gotten, he putteth spurres, and away as fast as the legges will carry. After him runneth the 'rest of the horsemen; and if they can overtake him, he summoneth a delivery of the knappan. If he hold the knappan it is lawful for the assaliant to beat him with the codgell till he deliver it. Now at this play privat grudges are revenged, soe that for every small occasion they fall by the eares, which being once kindled between two, all persons of both sides become parties . . . You shall see gamesters returne home from the playe, with broaken heads, black faces, brused bodies, and lame legges, yet laughing and jesting at their harmes." A strenuous game indeed, and a weird folk custom! Here in Wales, although the association is with the Easter season, rather than with weddings, as in the Cornish hurling, there is a definite similarity with one another, and with the French *la soule*. And the likeness is not only in the method of play, but also in the vestige of the old fertility rite.

The Scottish game of shinty, or *camanachd* is the north British form of hurling, but here resuming the resemblance to hockey, for it is played with a *caman*, or club. Descriptions of shinty, with its rough and tumble, fierce club fights are so similar to knappan and hurling, that it is not necessary to quote them. It has been claimed that shinty came to Scotland by way of Ireland, but so far the evidence is not conclusive. In Irish mythology Cuchulainn, Fionn, and Fingall play huge club and ball games over the land of the Gaels, and many are the mythological men who are proficient with ball and club. Allowing for the fact that these legends date back hundreds of years B.C., we must again remember that they were *written* A.D. The highly imaginative, romantic, legendary accounts should not be taken as historical sources.

It is of interest to note that the great shinty matches of Scotland were played on the winter holidays, especially on New Year's Day. Reminiscent of the *Seigneurs* of France in the middle ages, and the game of *la soule,* we read that "In Glenmoriston the laird and his sons, as well as the leading men, not only patronized the play, but also took a personal part in it." And again the old division by parishes: "Two sides of a parish, or two parishes, or two clan septs often engaged with one another on New Year's Day. Plenty of hard knocks were given and received, and—tell it not in the temperance hall—much *aqua-vitae* or *uisge-beatha,* went round, little of which had payed toll to the Crown. Till late in the 18th century it used to be played to and from the Church, but the wave of puritan piety that rolled over the Highlands about 1750 put an end to Sunday shinty."

Shinty is of special interest to us, because a secondary form of the game was played, in which the opposing sides had to drive the ball into a series of holes, again a possible source of golf.

14. Racquets

ALTHOUGH the modern game of racquets owes much to the enthusiasm of the Fleet Street debtors who played it for over one hundred years, the popular belief that the game originated in the Fleet Street Prison about the beginning of the nineteenth century, is erroneous both as to time and place.

In the volume on *Rackets, Squash Rackets, Tennis, Fives & Badminton,* in the *Lonsdale Library,* published in 1933, is the statement that it is "impossible to find a single reference to rackets before 1800," while Al Leney, in the *New York Herald Tribune* of January 12, 1936, states that "historians have been able to find no reference to racquets earlier than 1800." Both insist, however, that the idea of the game must go further back into history. It does.

The failure of historians of the game to recognize earlier material arises from the fact that prior to 1800 the name of the game was always in the singular form—"racket." After the year 1800 the plural form, "rackets" or "racquets" has usually been used, and now is the accepted form. Examples of the singular form after the turn of the century are not uncommon, for example in: Jon Bee's *Sportsman's Slang,* 1825; *The Fancy: or, True Sportsman's Guide,* 1826, and quite late in J. R. Atkins' *The Book of Racquets,* 1872, wherein the author repeatedly refers to "the game of racquet."

A note on the spelling of "racquet" may be in order. Since tennis and other racquet games had their distant origins in the Egyptian-Arabic-Persian *locale,* we might expect the words connected with the games to stem from oriental roots. Both "tennis" and "racquets" undoubtedly belong to this group. "Racquet" comes from the Arabic *ruqat,* meaning a patch of cloth, wound around the hand to protect it, and hence the earliest form of a racquet. This Arabic root, with its difficulties in transliteration, perhaps accounts for the wide variance in the spelling of "racquet," when it finally reached England.

The spelling "rackets" is favored in England, and "racquets" in the United States. The argument for "rackets" is usually based on a passage in Chaucer's *Troilus and Cressida:*

> But canstow playen raket to and fro
> Nettle in, dokke out, now this, now that, Pandare?

Unfortunately Chaucer spelled the word "raket," not "racket," the latter appearing in the printed editions some two hundred years after Chaucer's time. Moreover, his reference has no connection with a racquet: the "raket" of Chaucer is a game of dice! "Racquet" is, and always has been used for the sporting term: "racket" is used for many terms, some most opprobrious. Why not separate the two and use "racquet" always in sports?

The earliest mention of the game of racquets so far located

Lawn Tennis as invented by Major Wingfield, 1873.

Site of First Lawn Tennis Court in America. *Camp Washington, now St. George, Staten Island.*

Racquets, called Fives, 1788.

is in *Devorit with Dreme,* a poem written about the year
1500, by William Dunbar:

> Sa mony rakkettis, sa mony ketche-pillaris,
> Sic ballis, sic nackettis, and sic tutivillaris.

Or, to translate the old Scotch:

> So many racquet-players, so many tennis-players,
> Such ball-players, such markers, such worthless persons.

This is noteworthy in that this earliest reference to the game
of racquets links it with tennis, even if neither is commend-
able in the eyes of the poet.

Another poetic mention is found in the year 1529, by Sir
David Lindsay, the Scottish poet-tutor to King James V of
Scotland. Because of political intrigues, the young king, at
the age of twelve years, had been taken from the careful instruction of Lindsay, and put into the hands of unscrupulous
guides, who endeavored to influence him in such a way as
to ruin his character:

> Sum gart hym raiffell at the rakcat;
> Sum harld hym to the hurly hakcat.

That is to say, some urged him to revel ("raiffell," presumably
gamble) at the game of racquets, where a low type of gamester was usually in attendance, while others carried him to
the "hurly hakcat," a schoolboy sport of sliding down a steep
hill.

A little caution is necessary here. Does the word "rakcat"
as used here mean the game of racquets, or is the reference
to "raket" the game of dice mentioned by Chaucer, Usk and
Lydgate? That the game of dice is not intended is certain,
for it is listed amongst other pastimes recommended by the
unworthy counsellors:

Thare was no play bot cartis and dyce;
And ay Schir flattre bure the pryce.

The question may also be asked: Did Lindsay imply tennis when he said "rakcat?" Again the answer is in the negative. Lindsay was familiar with tennis under its Scottish name "the caiche," as witness his *Ane Satyre:*

Thocht I preich not, I can play at the caiche.

It may be assumed then, that when the author wrote "rakcat," he meant some forerunner, or perhaps nebulous form of the game of racquets.

In John Heywood's *The Four P.P.*, written in 1540, the Pardoner gives an entertaining description of the Nether Regions, where racquets was played by the imps of Satan, not with the usual instruments, but with firebrands:

The Master-Devil sat in his jacket,
And all the souls were playing at racket.
None other rackets they had in hand,
Save every soul a good firebrand.

Wherewith they played so prettily,
That Lucifer laughed merily;
And all the residue of the fiends
Did laugh thereat full well like friends.

John Guillim, in his *Display of Heraldry*, published in 1610, but still of great usefulness to the genealogist, has a chapter concerning the use as armorial bearings of "the arts of second rank, which tend rather to the embellishing and beautifying of nature's works, than to the necessary supply of human needs . . . Arts of delight, which are called playing: which comprehendeth either theatrical recreation, or other games whatsoever . . . Such are table playing, chess, dice, the racket . . ." and mentions the coat of arms of Jacobus Medices, "whose device was a ball with two balloons," and the inspiring motto, *Percussus elevor:* The harder I am stricken, the higher I mount."

The *New English Dictionary,* in quoting some of the above citations, refers to the game of "racket: a game played by two persons, who strike the ball alternately with their rackets, and endeavor to keep it bounding from a wall. Now always plural," but the early games were obviously played by more than two persons.

A certain popularity of racquets in the seventeenth century is indicated by James Howell, who, in a sarcastic allusion to the young fops of his day (1642), says: "Another when at the racket court he had a ball struck into his hazard, hee would ever and anon cry out, *estes vous lá avec vos Ours,* Are you there with your Beares?" And in 1652 John Taylor spoke of less formal games: "There is no such zeal in many places and Parishes of Wales; for they have neither service, prayer, sermon, minister or preacher, nor any church door opened at all, so that the people do exercise and edify in the churchyard at the lawful and laudable games of trap, cat, stool-ball, racket, &c. on Sundays."

Other early writers may also be noted: In one of Thomas Middleton's *Father Hubburd's Tales* (1604), the Ant relates how his master "was all day a courtier in the tennis-court" instead of at his books, and who, when reminded of the adage, *nulla dies sina linea,* remarked: "True . . . I observe it well, for I am no day from the line of the racket court." Again, in John Ogilby's *Aesop* (1651), we find the couplet:

> "Like Racket-Bals with Argos's I sport,
> And the whole Ocean is my Tennis-Court."

These last two quotations may perhaps arouse a question as to the use of the words "racket" and "tennis." In both cases they seem to be interchangeable. Are they synonymous, and in all cases is the game of tennis implied? J. R. Atkins is of the opinion that "both games have so much in common that it is impossible to separate them historically; for practical purposes we must regard them as identical." There is no doubt that the two games were closely associated. The definition of *Racket* as given by B. E., *Gent.*, in his *New Dictionary of the Terms . . . of the Canting Crew*, published in 1698 perhaps gives some weight to this point: "Racket . . . Also tennis play." But although closely associated, the two games were not identical.

Further evidence indicating that the two games, racquets and tennis were played in the old tennis courts is found in *The Double Distress: a tragedy*, by Mary Pix, and published in 1701. The Prologue to this play refers to the use of tennis courts for dramatic productions, a custom well established in France, where it was used by Molière, although not so general in England. *The Double Distress* was produced in The Tennis Court Theatre, Bear Yard, Little Lincoln's Inn Field —formerly known as Gibbon's Tennis Court, and converted to theatrical purposes in the days of Charles II. Says the Prologue:

> *Well, we've shew'n all we can to make you easie . . .*
> *If all won't do we must to Treat incline . . .*
> *'Tis quickly done, the Racket Walls remain.*
> *Give us but only time to shift the Scene,*
> *And Presto, we're a Tennis Court again.*

Mrs. Pix in using the term "Racket Walls" undoubtedly referred to the game of racquets, played in a tennis court.

John Armitage says that "it is foolish to suppose that the idea of the game originated in the minds of some poor debtors in . . . the Fleet Street Prison," and insists that it must have been of earlier origin. Let us then trace back a little. The earliest games of racquets were played against one wall only. Games in the Fleet were so played, as were the games played at certain ale houses, and the earlier games at the public schools in England. Ackermann's *Microcosm of London* (1808) contains a fine colored plate by Rowlandson, showing a game of racquets in progress within prison walls, and there are several other delineations of the sport played with one wall.

The Fleet Street Prison of Rowlandson and Dickens was built in 1781-1782, after the older prison had been destroyed in 1780. Even in the older prison the game was played. Howard's *State of the Prisons of England,* a report written in 1776, describes how the prisoners of the Fleet "also play in the court at skittles, mississippi, fives and tennis." This reference to tennis is puzzling. There certainly was no elaborate court necessary for the real game. Perhaps a rough game of tennis was attempted occasionally with only a "main wall," but an old print, earlier than Howard, suggests that the game witnessed by him was actually racquets.

Mention should be made here of a misleading print, *"Rackets in the Fleet,"* supposed to have been published by Bowles and Carver in 1760, and reproduced by John Ashton in his *The Fleet,* New York, 1888. According to the authorities at the British Museum, no print exists bearing the above title, published by Bowles and Carver. The print reproduced by Ashton is really *Fives, Played at the Tennis-Court, Leicester*

Fields, Printed and Sold by Carington Bowles in 1788, with the background omitted.

The earliest reference to racquets in the Fleet Prison, so far located, is a most interesting pamphlet, *The Humours of the Fleet: an Humourous and Descriptive Poem, Written by a Gentleman of the College.* This pamphlet leaves no doubt that racquets was in full swing as early as the year 1749, when it was published. The poem describes The Fleet,

> *Within whose ample Oval is a Court*
> *Where the more active and Robust resort,*
> *And glowing, exercise a Manly sport.*
> *(Strong exercise with mod'rate food is Good,*
> *It drives in Sprightful Streams the circling blood;*
> *While these with Rackets strike the manly Ball.)*

The poem is illustrated with a cut showing the courtyard, in the background of which may be seen a game of racquets in progress against the prison wall. Although the reference in the text is to the implement, the illustration, together with the text, clearly establishes the fact that the game is racquets.

Now, if a large wall were needed to play racquets, what more natural place to play than in a tennis court? As to this, Julian Marshall flatly states: "The game of rackets originated in a tennis court," and refers to the print *Fives, Played in the Tennis Court, Leicester Fields,* 1788, in support of his conclusion. The print shows a game of racquets, in a tennis court, one wall of which has been marked to show the bounds wherein the ball must stay. "Despite its title," says John Armitage, "this picture depicts a game of Rackets."

The 1749 print in *The Humours of the Fleet* shows the game of racquets to be in existence before the Leicester Fields print of 1788, but the latter print does establish the

Racquets played in the old Fleet Street Prison, 1749.

fact that racquets and fives (for there is little difference between the two games) were played in tennis courts. Since
admittance to The Fleet was not a prerequisite to all who
wished to play the game, it is reasonable to suppose that
racquets was played in tennis courts before and after it became popular in The Fleet. Recently the writer asked an old
tennis professional if he had ever seen a game of racquets
played in a tennis court, and was surprised to receive the
answer: "Yes, I was doing that very thing myself this morning!" It is highly probable that some tennis-racquets players,
incarcerated in the Debtors' Prison bethought themselves of
their erstwhile pastime, and introduced the game to the place
of their confinement.

99

The seeming synonymity of the terms racquet and tennis, therefore, arises from the fact that both games were played in the same places. The Ant referred to a tennis-court at the beginning of a sentence, and finished with a racket-court. It was both. It is not a case of two terms for one game, but of two games in the same place.

It may be safely concluded that the game of racquets, formerly called "racket," has existed in England since the year 1500, not long after the racquet began to be in general use. It originated in the early tennis courts, and was played in somewhat formless fashion, without set rules, until the eighteenth century, when it became the pastime of the inmates of The Fleet Street Prison. By the year 1749 the game was well established. After the erection of the new Fleet Street Prison in 1782, racquets achieved such popularity that its fame spread beyond The Fleet. It began to be played in saloons, and other nondescript places, and finally was taken up by the "public" schools, the large private schools of England, soon after the middle of the nineteenth century. The game was then enclosed within four walls, and attained respectability. Thus, while the game did not start in The Fleet, its development, if not its present existence as a game, is due to the fact that the prisoners detained there found it to be such a diverting pastime.

15. Racquets in America

THE history of bat and ball games on the American continent has never been adequately recorded. The colonists may have had inclination to play, but they had little encouragement, and less time: their religious mentors frowned upon such worldly activities, and the medicos had not yet taught the benefits of exercise. Yet forms of tennis and racquets (also known as fives) were undoubtedly played at comparatively early dates.

For instance, there is the proclamation of Governor Peter Stuyvesant of New York, in the year 1659. A "Day of universal Fasting and Prayer" was set for October 15th, "solemnly to call on the Lord's name . . . to remove from our road His just plagues, wherewith we are already stricken," and on that day were forbidden "all exercise and games of tennis, ball playing," and other sundry pastimes. Evidently tennis must have been popular with some classes in Stuyvesant's time, for it heads the lists of amusements. But no other records, names of players, or details of the game have been found.

It is known that racquets was played at Halifax in Nova

101

Scotia at the time of the American Revolution. Probably it had been introduced some time earlier, but the records are blank—or unlocated.

Racquets was played in New York City prior to the revolution. In those days the tavern played a large part in the life of the community: it was the place for political and social gatherings, and it is in connection with a tavern that we find the first games of racquets in New York. Martin Prendergast owned a tavern, "The Sign of the Hurlers, between the New-Gaol and Fresh Water Hill," which was in the neighborhood of what is now Leonard Street, west of Broadway. Martin Prendergast had added, as one of the attractions to his tavern "a very fine Tennis-Court, or Fives-Alley," and there racquets, or fives, was played. Just when this racquets court was built is unknown, but it was offered "To be sold at Publick Vendue, on Friday 29th of April," 1763. At that time the tavern stood on the outskirts of the city, in a section not laid out in streets.

The name of only one player in this tavern racquets court has been preserved. A man named Lowery many years later, when of advanced age, was made an honorary member of the Allen Street Court because, in spite of his age, he still remained an expert at the game. It was supposed that Lowery had learned his racquets in England.

The players at "The Sign of the Hurlers" possibly purchased their supplies from James Rivington, in New York City, for in the year 1766 he advertised for sale, imported, "best racquets for tennis and fives."

Racquets seems to have temporarily disappeared from New York shortly after the sale of the Prendergast tavern. Its re-introduction came by way of Halifax, Nova Scotia, and was a by-product of the revolution.

James Knox had come to America from Paisley, in Scotland. His loyalty to the British Crown remained unaffected by the colonial insurrectionists, for when hostilities broke out between the colonies and the mother country in 1776, he fled to Halifax. There he saw the game of racquets, played it, and at once became an enthusiastic lover of the sport.

When peace had been re-established James Knox returned to New York, and was instrumental in establishing a racquets court later known as the Allen Street Court. This was on a lot at 25 Orchard Street, reaching through to 24 Fourth Street, which in 1817, became Allen Street. Allen and Orchard Streets ran between Walker (which became Pump in 1829, and Canal in 1855) and Eagle Street (which later became Hester).

The exact date and circumstances of the erection of the court are uncertain. James Knox probably returned to New York City after 1783. A James Knox, lumber merchant, had a place of business at the corner of The Bowery and Eagle (Hester) not far from Allen Street in 1796. In 1799 he was located at Orchard Street, where he evidently bought the lot extending from Orchard to Allen about that time, and built the court in 1800. In 1803 he is listed in the city directory as "Tavern and Ball Alley Orchard," but in 1804 and thereafter he is listed as "Ball Alley" only.

According to Edward La Montagne, writing in 1901, Knox's court was "100 feet long by 36 feet wide; there was no back wall, but simply lines on the floor. The service was from a ring in the centre of the court; one had to serve over the line which crossed the ring 30 feet from the front wall, then inside a back line about 80 feet from the front wall. Service was good only when within these lines."

The recollection of Montagne, some fifty years after the old court had disappeared, is not very reliable: his figures must not be taken as they stand. An old engraving of the court showing the lines as described suggests a much shorter court. The length of the entire lot from Allen to Orchard, according to contemporary maps, was 175 feet at most. Since the court with the club house occupied "about half a lot," the entire length of the building was not more than 90 feet. The line with the ring was "in the centre of the court," but also "30 feet from the front wall," which would make the court 60 feet in length. Probably the absence of an end wall, and extra space in front of the court gave the impression of additional length.

The district around Allen Street at that time was being newly developed, and soon became one of the best residential sections of the city. It is evident that socially prominent men who lived in the neighborhood became interested in Knox's tavern, and speedily converted it into a club, where they could obtain a little exercise at racquets, relaxation at whist, and meet congenial spirits. Knox seems to have remained as proprietor. No distinctive name appears to be attached to the court, except that of Knox himself. But membership in the group was strictly limited to "the old Knickerbocker and most aristocratic families of the city." At least that was the intention. That exceptions were made to this rule will become evident later.

The Allen Street Court rightly may be considered the forerunner of The Racquet and Tennis Club. True, there was no *official* connection between the Allen Street Court and the Racket Court Club of 1845, and that, in turn, had no *official* connection with the Racquet Court Club of 1875, which merged into the Racquet and Tennis Club of 1890. Yet members of the same families, for almost one hundred and forty years, have been the constant supporters of these sporting clubs, and the leading exponents of the game of racquets. Continuity may be claimed on the ground of family and social ties and interest, if not on the ground of continuity of organization.

The building of the Allen Street Court was a two story frame house, simple in design, with no attempt at architectural embellishment. It stood back some distance from the street. Along the front of the lot ran a fence, through which members entered through a gate of unplaned boards, which swung on barn door hinges. A sash weight attached to the end of a cord that ran over a pulley served as a self-closing device.

The building at the back of the club house was a doubles court, larger than the present regulation size. The end wall was said to be sixty feet in height, with side walls sloping down to lower than forty feet. The court was built of brick, faced with brown stone. The floor was made of the best boards obtainable, put together by the most skillful carpenters in the city. The court had no roof, consequently, when it rained, those who wanted to play racquets were obliged to wait until the court dried.

The club house itself, which was only one room deep, faced the front of the court: indeed it was built directly against it. The "dressing room" downstairs was somewhat primitive: it contained lockers for clothing, and a pump which was the sole water supply. A plain wooden trough was the common receptacle for members' valuables when they went to play. Watches, rings and money, wrapped in neat little parcels, were put in that simple "safe."

The one room upstairs was called the "Whist Room," but also served the many and sundry purposes of a club. It was the social gathering place of the club. In winter time, when inclement weather probably reduced to slim numbers the ranks of the racquets players, a Franklin stove warmed the Whist Room. A crude table filled one corner, on which could always be found a tray of tumblers and decanters of the finest gin and brandy in the city. These drinks were free to members, but champagne sold for two dollars a bottle, while Havana cigars sold for five cents apiece.

The simplicity of the club house may be imagined from the fact that the stairs which led up to the Whist Room boasted no hand rail. After the club had been in existence for many years, one of the members, Thaddeus Phelps, missed his footing and broke his leg, whereupon a rope was stretched from the top to the bottom of the stair to prevent a repetition of the occurrence. Nevertheless, after an evening at whist, when any member started for home, it became the invariable custom for him to be lighted down the hazardous way by a fellow member with a candle. Candles, incidentally, were used for lighting the building: but they were not ordinary candles. They were imported sperm candles, and the silver candlesticks which held them gave, perhaps, the one touch of elegance to the otherwise simple club, and a prophetic glimpse of the splendours of later club houses.

The organization of the Allen Street club seems to have been very simple. In all probability the property was leased from James Knox, who retained supervision over the building. There is no record of a governing committee of any kind, although some such committee may have existed. The club was presided over by a Chancellor, who combined the authority of a czar with the wisdom of a Solomon. He acted upon controversies over whist or racquets, when these matters were brought to him for settlement. He would hold a most informal hearing, listening to the arguments of each side, which were always carried on as though they were sporting events in themselves. The Chancellor's decision would then be rendered, and usually the loser was fined a bottle of wine. The records do not make clear who got the bottle, but no doubt the Chancellor and the two disputants readily solved the problem of its disposal.

Ferguson Livingston was the first Chancellor, indeed the only one recorded during the existence of the club. It is not known if he held office for the entire period, or if others succeeded him. A few names of members are noted, but they are probably of a later rather than an earlier period. These include Robert Emmet, Thomas Addis Emmet, Gideon Potts, Henry Coit, William Bradford, Philip Hone, John Hone, Henry Hone, Commodore Vanderbilt, Hugh Maxwell, Jesse Hoit, Amos Palmer, Thaddeus Phelps, Henry Suydam, Richard Suydam, Herman Leroy, Isaac Townsend (father of the Isaac Townsend who became President of the Racquet and Tennis Club), Gabriel Wisner, Anthony Wisner, Anthony Winans, Charles Livingston, "and practically all the male members of the Schermerhorn, Leroy and Pendleton families."

In the early days no special costume was worn when members exercised at racquets. Each member kept on hand an old pair of trousers and a change of linen. This is rather strange, for the necessity of special dress of the sweat-absorbent type

107

had been recognized as long ago as the sixteenth century, when tennis court keepers supplied appropriate garb, which went with the rental of the court by players. But the Allen Street men did let themselves out when it came to footwear. They wore elaborate moccasins of a peculiar pattern, made of buckskin. The soft tops came up well over the ankle, and then turned down in a roll, which gave a natty finish. The soles were thick, and the entire effect was very ornate.

A box containing powdered resin stood at the entrance to the court, and members were wont to put the resin on the soles of their moccasins before playing to prevent slipping.

The racquets used at Allen Street were strong, heavy affairs. They could stand hard use, but required a man in good training to handle.

The balls were of a very fine quality, made of white woolen yarn, dampened and wound tightly around a piece of solid rubber about the size of a marble. They were covered with white kid, and sewed with silk of various colors: blue, yellow and scarlet. A box of balls was a pretty sight.

James Knox remained actively interested in the management of the Allen Street court until his death in 1818, when he was succeeded by his son Robert Knox. The son does not appear to have made much impression, for all that is recorded of him is that he conducted the affairs of the club until his decease in 1826, but he did transmit to his son, in turn, a love of the game of racquets, for Robert Knox II became the outstanding player of his time in the eighteen forties.

Peter Hurley was born in Belleville, N. J. in the year 1804, and came to live with the Knoxes in 1821. Upon the death of the first Robert Knox he took over the property, and remained in charge of the club until its sale about the year 1850. In

1876, when the Racquet Court Club was organized, Hurley was living in retirement in the Morrisania section of the city, and was known as "one of the oldest, if not the oldest racket champion in the country." When the new club opened, a reporter from the New York *Sun* sought him out, and it is due to Hurley's reminiscences as reported on this occasion that we owe much of our knowledge of the early history of the game in New York City.

There is no record of the members of the Allen Street Court, but by the eighteen thirties there must have been a couple of hundred. They were elected by acclamation, paid no initiation fee, and the dues, which they cheerfully paid, amounted to but ten dollars a year. There were no markers or other professionals: members did their own calling, besides paying for the privilege of playing.

The influx of new members encouraged the club to enlarge its quarters, and at some time, probably after 1830, a brick building was erected on the front part of the lot. The picturesque fence and its wooden gate gave way to the new building.

The addition was much more pretentious than the old building, although, restricted by the size of the lot, it also consisted of two rooms, one upstairs and one down. The upper room was devoted to billiards, while the lower room was an "up-to-date" dressing room. It had lockers to hold not only clothing and racquets, but sufficiently safe to make obsolete the old wooden trough which had for many years been the strong box of the club. But the greatest improvement was the provision of wash basins with running water, which replaced the old-fashioned pump.

The sporting reporter was not much in evidence during

Chancellor Livingston's regime, and there are few records to games played. On one occasion Robert Fulton visited the court as the guest of Walter Livingston. He watched a game of doubles for a while, but was unimpressed with his first contact with racquets. "Nothing to it," he thought, and ventured the opinion that he could beat any of the four players on the court. Accordingly, Livingston selected the poorest of the four players, and matched him with Fulton, with a bottle of wine as the stake. Much to his astonishment and chagrin Fulton was easily beaten. "Well," said he, "this deuced game of ball has deceived me more than any of my steamboat schemes ever did."

On another occasion Lord John Hay, then an officer in the British navy, and another Englishman "of renown at the game" visited the club, and the latter played against Peter Hurley. Hurley gave a handicap, limiting himself to the use of a broom handle instead of a racquet, but in spite of this won easily.

In the 1840's Robert Knox II, grandson of the original James Knox, was the outstanding player. For many years he was unbeatable, and remained champion of the club until the advent of the redoubtable Edward La Montagne. The Montreal Racket Club organized in 1836, and La Montagne joined it in 1838. He was champion of the Montreal club until he came to New York in 1848, when he met Robert Knox and wrested the New York championship from him.

Among other prominent players at Allen Street were Samuel Swartwout, Collector of the Port of New York, Elizur Davis, Thomas D. Howes and William Devoe.

Contemporary with the Allen Street Court in New York was another racquets court at the corner of the Bowery and

Broome Street. It was operated by Alexander Fink, and because it was patronized largely by butchers, was known as the "Butchers' Club." The butchers must have been lusty fellows, for in 1833 their champion, William Harrington, handsomely beat Benjamin R. Theall of the Allen Street club, in spite of the fact that during the game Harrington carried on his back a man weighing 175 pounds. Another member of the Butchers' Club was Elias De Forrest, better known as Uncle Elias, who had the reputation of being a fine player, and sure hitter.

Shortly after 1840 a feeling of dissatisfaction was evident amongst some of the members of the Allen Street club, and a small group, led by Robert Emmet, considered the possibility of a new organization.

The basis of the complaint was the admittance to the court of "uncongenial" visitors, who made themselves objectionable in that they frequented the court not to play, but to gamble, and they encouraged inordinately high stakes. The new organization's success could "only be secured by a strict adherence to the restrictions upon gambling, and rules governing the admission of members and strangers to be introduced by them."

The objection to gambling in the racquets courts was well advised, for history shows that it has always mitigated against the best interests of the games of racquets and tennis. In Italy, in the seventeenth century, the courts suffered by the unwelcome presence of gamblers. "The stake motive of the ancients," a contemporary writer protested, "is not identical with that of the moderns. With the former, winning was a sort of wholesome fun, with no eye to lucre. Nor did those who lost feel it keenly, for the stakes put up by each player

111

were not over 4 or 5 dinars, by no means an excessive amount. The modern ball players, however, may win or lose sums that are considerable, and diversion is not their primary object, but material gain." The many allusions to the matter in English literature of the seventeenth and eighteenth centuries, particularly in *The Country Gentleman's Vade-Mecum*, of 1699, leave no doubt that the evil reputation associated with racquets and tennis courts, because of their misuse by the gambling fraternity, did much to cause their temporary disappearance. And so, when the new club was started, strong measures were taken to prevent a recurrence of the trouble. The organization committee unanimously agreed that an infraction of the rule restricting gambling would involve the forfeiture of membership without appeal, and the rule was duly incorporated in the new constitution.

The men who seceded from the Allen Street Court with Robert Emmet included E. Boonen Graves, Samuel Whitney and Beverly Robinson. So determined were the members of the new organization to maintain high standards of membership, that they would not admit tradespeople to membership. Some of the best citizens in mercantile circles were proposed as members, but were blackballed, and one of the unfortunates who came under the ban was the famous New Yorker, A. T. Stewart.

Not long afterwards, discouraged by the secession of its ablest supporters, the old Allen Street Court sold its property, and about the year 1850 it was demolished.

The new group obtained considerable impetus when Richard F. Carman offered to construct a club house for their use, and on the 24th of February, 1845—the same year that Alexander J. Cartwright modernized the old game of baseball—

the Racquet Court Club was organized. This club, which formally opened its building at 594 Broadway, existed until the year 1855. In 1854, in anticipation of the sale of the building which housed the Racket Court Club, the families interested in racquets formed The Gymnasium Club, which had a two-story structure on Thirteenth Street, where it remained until 1868. One more attempt to keep racquets going in New York was made with The Racquet Court Club in 1875, which reorganized finally into the Racquet and Tennis Club, in 1890. Here the game stayed and prospered. Its Club House at 370 Park Avenue is now one of New York's finest Clubs.

16. Golf

GOLF is the national game of Scotland and has been called "Scotland's gift" to mankind. But is it Scottish? On this point argument has been endless, for the proponents of a Dutch origin are many. The question is better understood if considered in the light of the theory of the common origin of bat and ball games. Of course golf differs from other games in that, while it is competitive, two sides do not attack the same ball: each player has his own. Is this feature enough to differentiate it, or to completely sever it, from all connection with other ball games? We think not.

We have seen how *la soule* was played early in the fourteenth century, first as a rough and tumble scramble for the ball, then as a game resembling hockey, but played in a variety of ways with variously shaped clubs or sticks. Quite early in Southern France *jeu de mail* developed, later known in the England of the Stuarts as pall mall, or pell mell. In this game two sides strove to drive a ball to a given mark in the least number of strokes. The mark was a stone, tree or other upright object. It was a long-driving, cross-country game. The boxwood ball, about the size of a lawn tennis ball, was driven with a mallet, a stick with a wooden head. During the

GOLF

fourteenth century the game of *jeu de mail* developed from the earlier traditional ball customs. In the chapter on polo a Byzantian game of *tzycanisterium* was shown to have a relationship to the old pagan rituals. Du Cange claims that this game of ball "owed its origin to the French, and that in the first place it was nothing else than the one which is still in use in Languedoc (that is, in 1668), called there *chicane*, and in other provinces the *mallet* game, *jeu de mail*." In Languedoc chicane was played in a flat field, or along highways.

In England *jeu de mail* reached considerable popularity amongst the wealthier classes early in the seventeenth century. Here a further modification was made. Just as *la soule* had been reduced to ground billiards, so pall mall was played on a definite "ground" and the ball had to be driven through an iron ring suspended in the air.

The earliest rules of *jeu de mail* were published in Paris by Joseph Lauthier in 1717, some forty years before the earliest rules of golf. It was played as recently as 1863 and probably later, in Montpellier, in France, where the characteristics of the countryside were utilized—another case of a game adapting itself to natural hazards. The country roads near Montpellier had high banks on either side, sometimes ditches or hedges. The surface of the roads were extremely rough and variable, even tortuous, all of which made many natural obstacles, giving much interest and variety as the ball was driven towards the chosen mark.

The translation of Lauthier's book, published by Andrew Lang in 1910, and also in R. C. A. Prior's *Notes on Croquet*, in 1872, describes details of the game. Instructions on the "stroke" might almost be taken for golf. The resemblance of the early form of *jeu de mail* to golf is great: to drive a ball to a given mark in the least number of strokes. But the mark was upright in *jeu de mail* instead of a series of holes as in golf.

We find a form of *la soule* played in Belgium as early as 1353 under the name of *choule* or *chole*, and it also spread through Flanders and Holland. This game, after its journey from France to Holland, as it did in so many other places, took on a local variation, evolving as the game of *kolven*. Early illustrations of *kolven* have led many to believe that golf had its origin in Holland. But mention of *kolven* during the fifteenth and sixteenth centuries in the works of Dutch writers are slight, and give no idea of how the game was played. We must rely entirely on the work of contemporary Dutch artists for our knowledge of the game, such as an illustration in a Flemish *Book of Hours* of about 1500 to 1520, and another illustration in the *Book of Hours* of the Duchess of Burgundy of 1560.

It was not until about 1700 that we have a detailed account of *kolven* as played in Holland. It was a cross-country game, an interesting variation from the older game of *chole*, although it still retained a slight association with the Church, and resembled very closely the *jeu de mail* of the French. Two sides opposed one another, playing with the *same* ball. The attacking side selected a distant mark a mile or more away, usually the door of a church or marketplace cross. The attacking side had to declare that it could drive the ball with its clubs (*kolven*) in a certain number of strokes to the selected mark. They started the game with three strokes in succession, after which the defending side took one stroke. This was a crucial stroke, for the defenders, whenever their turn to strike the ball came, would drive the ball backwards, at the same time endeavouring to drive it into as difficult a "bunker" as might be within reach. Halma's Dutch dictionary of 1708 relates how "they make a little heap of sand or snow on which they place the ball, and thus striking it underneath, they can send it a great distance to a distant mark or goal." This comparatively recent description still refers to "the mark," with no mention of a "hole."

Chole, and later *kolven* in Holland, as in other countries was the popular game of the country people: its requirement of plenty of space necessitated a thinly populated countryside. But when the townspeople took it up trouble began. Damage to property was common and public safety was at stake, and so the game was prohibited in the streets. Following this it became a winter sport exclusively, played on the frozen canals and ponds, as many of the artists of the time portrayed. Here again the object of the game was to drive the ball to an upright mark.

It was not until 1657 that we find *kolven* described at length in Dutch literature, in the comedy of *Moortje* by Bredero, a poet of Amsterdam. The translation by Martin Hardie, made for H. H. Hilton's *The Royal and Ancient Game of Golf* reads:

> *The golfer binds his ice-spurs on,*
> *Or something stiff to stand upon.*
> *For the smooth ice all snowless lying*
> *Laughs and jests at polished soles.*
> *Sides drawn by lot, the golfer stands,*
> *Ready to smite with ashen club*
> *Weighted with lead, or his Scottish club*
> *Of leaded box, three fingers broad, one thick,*
> *The feather ball, invisible from drive to fall*
> *By fore-caddies is keenly marked*
> *As he golfs forwards to a limit post,*
> *Or strikes for the furthest, stroke against stroke,*
> *At a white mark, or flag in the hole.*

Is the Dutch *kolven* the source of Scottish golf? No. *Kolven* is a descendant, through the Belgian *chole*, of the French *la soule*. It appears to be a refinement of *jeu de mail*, or at least a variation of it, both games examples of local adaptations of the ancient Easter ball games. Up to the sixteenth century we only have pictorial representations of *kolven*, and these illustrations indicate a mark set up to be played for, rather than a hole in the ground, and sometimes within a circumscribed area. The Bruges *Book of Hours* of 1560 seems to be a solitary exception. It is Flemish, but may be taken as representative of the low-countries. There is no other early evidence of a hole-game, all other references being to an upright mark. It has been suggested that the artist of the Bruges book was familiar with Scottish golf and thus added a hole, which was quite a possibility. But any resemblance between *kolven* and golf is superficial.

How, then, did golf originate in Scotland? We have already noted a relationship, if not identity, between the Scottish shinty, Cornish hurling and French *la soule*. Alexander McBain describes two forms of shinty, one named *camanachd*, from the hooked stick or *caman* with which it is played, and which resembles hockey. The other "side form of shinty" had as its leading feature "the getting of the ball into a series of holes (in old time called "poll" or "toll"). Both McBain and J. N. Macdonald state that this distinction between the two forms of Shinty goes back to ancient Ireland: both claim that it was from the hole-game of shinty that golf sprang. We have also noted a variation of Shrove Tuesday ball games in Scone, Scotland, in which the object of the married men was to put the ball three times into a small hole in the moor. This form of the game is described in 1796, but we have no evidence to say when the hole-game was first played in Scone. Shinty pre-dates golf, and the form played with holes might very well have been a forerunner of golf. Another Scottish historian, "A Golfer," in his *Historical Gossip about Golf and Golfers,* in 1863 concluded: "We think it more likely—and we have seen nothing to make us think otherwise—that golf had its origin in our own Scotch game of shinty." With this conclusion the present writer agrees. Ball games as a whole slowly evolved elsewhere in a multitude of local variations, well-established folk customs. It is reasonable to suppose that golf also developed gradually through traditional customs, and shinty is a logical ancestor of golf.

Golf came into the scene about the fourteenth or beginning of the fifteenth century. In 1424 the King of Scotland prohibited football and other games, but made no mention of golf, whereas in 1457 James II "decreeted and ordained that the fute-ball and golfe be utterly cryit doune . . . and that the bow merkis be maid at ilk paroche kirk . . . ilk Sunday." The inclusion of golf in a list of games which interfered with proficiency in archery in 1457 may be held to indicate its popularity at that time. Similar prohibitions were made in 1471, 1491 and later. In 1618 the importation of golf balls from the continent was prohibited. Then, of course, we find the familiar Sabbath Day prohibitions, such as the 1592 Edinburgh ordinance "that seeing the Sabboth day being the Lord's day it becumis everie Christiane to dedicate himselff to the Service of God . . . na inhabitants . . . be sene at ony pastimes or gammis . . . sic as Golf." But James VI of Scotland (James I of England) rebuked the "precise people" and declared "that after the end of Divine Service, our good people be not disturbed" from such recreations. Although golf has been played continuously in Scotland since the fifteenth century, the oldest surviving code is the *Articles and Code of Playing Golf, St. Andrews, 1754,* which listed but thirteen rules.

A ball made of feathers has caused some discussion amongst historians of golf. The country people of ancient Rome played with a *paganica,* a ball made of leather stuffed with feathers. The Dutch and the Scotch used a similar ball, thus suggesting a connection between the ancient Roman games and golf. But there is none. O. P. Monckton has summed up the matter of the feather ball: "Golf is almost certainly a derivative from one of those early ball games of which the *ludum pilae celebrem* (celebrated ball game) of Fitzstephen was a precursor; but to give the game any greater antiquity than the fourteenth century would be to err on the extreme side of improbability, in spite of the feather nature of the ball." We would trace golf back to shinty, from shinty through Cornish and Irish hurling, and back through *la soule* to the ancient Egyptian folk-fertility rites. But the development of the game itself is Scottish.

17. Billiards

IT perhaps may seem odd to group the game of billiards with such robust out-of-door games as hockey, football, tennis and baseball. Nevertheless billiards is also a direct descendant of the old Egyptian fertility rites, a close relative of these other games.

The game of *jeu de mail* was first mentioned in the *Chansons de Roland* in the twelfth century. It has already been mentioned as a source of the Dutch *kolven. Jeu de mail* was a cross-country ball-hitting game and is undoubtedly a form of *la soule*, taking on characteristics caused by the natural hazards of the country-side in Southern France. From *jeu de mail* in turn sprang two other popular games, one croquet, the other *jeu de boules* which later developed into billiards.

About the year 1460 a famous French tapestry known as *Les amours de Gombaut et de Macée* was made. It was first inventoried at St. Lô in 1532. This tapestry portrayed scenes around the country-side at St. Lô, two of which show a game called *jeu de boules ou de tiquet*. A small ground is enclosed in a low wattle fence. Within the enclosure, at some distance from each other, appear an arch, or low hoop, later called a "port," and a small cone-shaped marker, later called a "king." Three players and three balls indicate that each played his own ball, and each player carries a mace, or cue, which appears to be a long wooden stick with a spade-shaped, slightly curved end.

Here we have a development of the game of *jeu de mail,* again affected by local temperament or individual fancy. The *crosse* of former days has become the spade-shaped stick. The less energetic, or perhaps the ladies, can now take part in a milder game. Since the natural hazards of roads, ditches and walls have been removed, substitute hazards are invented in the "port" through which the ball must be driven, and the cone-shaped "king" which must not be knocked over as the ball travels around it. *Jeu de boules* is none other than the link between *jeu de mail,* as played on the ground, and the modern game of billiards, played on a table. The game was also called *billard de terre,* or ground billiards, a name which indicates a definite relationship. One other feature of this fifteenth century game justifies the claim that it was an ancestor of billiards: the ball could be caromed off the sides of the enclosure, which were commonly made of planks of wood.

The next step was *le billard monté,* so called when the small enclosure was first raised on legs and became a table. Some claim that billiards was invented by Henrique de Vigne, about the year 1571 when he designed the first table at the request of Henry III of France, for his summer place, the Chateau de Blois, but this claim is not too well substantiated. Undoubtedly the new table game was an adaptation of the older out-of-doors ground billiards, for the earliest illustrations of the games show an amazing similarity, if not identity. The iron port and cone-shaped king both appear on the raised table, and in both cases the balls are pushed with the end of identically shaped spade-like maces. The engraving made by A. Trouvain of Louis XIV of France playing billiards (which he did on the advice of his physician), as late as 1674, still has the port and king, with no change in the mace. In the same year, however, another illustration of the Duchess of Burgundy playing billiards adds a hole in one corner, with ladies in waiting carrying additional maces.

Strutt states that during the seventeenth century the table was square, but his illustration, taken from *The School of Recreation* of 1710, is merely a redrawing from Cotton's *Compleat Gamester* of 1674. The table, in perspective, is rectangular, not square. It does have three pockets, all on one side, as well as the older arched port and cone-shaped king. By 1700 the port and king had disappeared and by 1734 the modern cue began to displace the spade-shaped mace. The earliest rules of billiards known to us today appeared in Cotton's *Compleat Gamester* which was published in 1674.

18. Lawn Tennis

OPINION as to the origin of lawn tennis, some seventy years after the event, seems to be unanimous, but at its inception there was much controversy. Claims and counter-claims were made, much like those which have attended baseball in America.

In the 1870's, in England, there was an awakening of interest in athletic sports. Polo had recently been introduced from India; the new game of badminton suddenly became popular; racquets, although still suffering from its associations with debtors' prisons, was an old game struggling for recognition in respectable society, and although the ancient game of court tennis was all but extinct, many people had old racquets and balls, and experimented in efforts to develop an outdoor racquet game. Lawn tennis, while owing most to the ancient court tennis, was a synthesis of this game with badminton and racquets.

As early as 1767 a London merchant, William Hickey, records with considerable gusto his membership in a Club of twenty members. "The game we played," he says, "was an invention of our own called field tennis. The Club consisted of

124

Cricket on the Artillery Ground, Finsbury, 1743.
From a painting by Francis Hayman.

Cricket played with curved stick, and Stoolball, 1744.

Allen Street Racquets Court, New York, built about 1800.

some very respectable persons . . . and met at the Red House in Battersea. Our regular meetings were two days each week, when we assembled at one o'clock. At two we sat down to dinner," which he describes in detail. It was Gargantuan. "At four our sport commenced, continuing until dark; during the exercise we refreshed ourselves with draughts of cool tankard and other pleasant beverages." Obviously the Club was a gay organization which took care of the social as well as athletic needs of a group of young blades. It is unfortunate that Hickey, in his diaries, should have had so much interest in describing the good times of the Club members to the neglect of the "Field tennis" which he failed to mention other than by name.

Of course the game of "long tennis," an outdoor tennis game modeled on court tennis, which had been played for many years in France, was bound to find its way to England and in 1834 Walker speaks of, and illustrates, a game of "field tennis" which closely resembled long tennis. A number of people in England in the 1860's and early 1870's had become interested in a game which was to become lawn tennis. "The game had several fathers," says A. E. Crawley, "Major Wingfield, James Lilywhite, 'J.R.H.C.,' 'G.C.C.,' Major Perera and J. H. Hale, with Cavendish (Henry Jones) as its Godfather, and three mothers—tennis, rackets and badminton."

After some experimentation, Major Walter Clopton Wingfield eventually arranged for a Christmas Party at Nantclwyd, in Wales, and for that occasion printed a little pamphlet called *The Major's Game of Lawn Tennis. Dedicated to the Party assembled at Nantclwyd in December, 1873.* The cover bore a Greek title: *Sphairistike, or Lawn Tennis.* Thus the first rules of the game of lawn tennis were published and the

125

credit for their formulation and for the name *Lawn Tennis* goes to Major Wingfield.

Wingfield's lawn tennis was played on a court shaped like an hour-glass, with a neat little diamond in the center of one court from which service was to be made. There were but six rules. The scoring was as in racquets, by aces, and the badminton touch is evident in advertisements of the game which soon appeared, which called it "Improved Wingless Tennis." Wingfield, insisting that the game was his invention, on February 23, 1874 took out a patent for a "new and improved portable court for playing the ancient game of tennis." This patent consisted of a net across the court, from the ends of which stretched triangular nets at either side, for a short distance down each side line. The court was the same hour-glass shape as in his book.

His action in claiming a patent stirred considerable protest, for already the game had "clicked" in the public imagination. Moreover, many men had had some part in perfecting the game, either independently or as friends of Wingfield. Many writers to the Editor of *The Field* stated that the game had been played in several places: at Ancrum in Roxburghe in 1864; at Leyton "for the last six years"; "years ago in Sussex, Surrey and Yorkshire" and particularly at the Leamington Club, where it was known as Lawn Tennis or Pelota.

Wingfield, however, insisted upon his "invention" until the day he died. But he was not mercenary and was most coöperative with those who sought to improve what was obviously a primitive game. The famous Marylebone Cricket Club was most interested. Many meetings were held, and on May 29, 1875, the Club issued new *Rules* "Revised by the M.C.C." These *Rules* the gallant Major graciously approved in a letter to *The Field* of June 5, 1875, and thus freed the game for popular enjoyment. The M.C.C. *Rules* immediately became "official" and formed the basis for subsequent revisions.

Shortly after this, J. M. Heathcote, tackling the problem of a too-light rubber ball, thought of adding a flannel cover to add weight without decreasing the resiliency of the ball: a simple enough device, but one that "made" the game of lawn tennis.

It is astonishing to note how fast the game of lawn tennis traveled to America. There has been some debate as to where and by whom it was introduced; it was formerly believed that the first court in America was laid out at Nahant, near Boston, in the summer of 1875 and that the first players were Dr. James Dwight and F. R. Sears, Jr. But Malcolm D. Whitman has proven conclusively that the honor of introducing the game of lawn tennis to America goes to Miss Mary E. Outerbridge. Wingfield brought out his book of rules and made sets available for purchase in England in December, 1873, although he did not take out his patent until February, 1874.

In the winter of 1873-1874, while on vacation in Bermuda, Miss Outerbridge observed some British Army officers playing lawn tennis. From them she obtained a set which, according to the manifest of the passenger steamer S.S. *Canima*, she brought with her to the Port of New York on February 2, 1874. Her brother, A. Emilius Outerbridge, who was a Director of the Staten Island Cricket Club, obtained permission from the Club for his sister to set up her net and mark out a court in one corner of the grounds, which she did in the spring of 1874. Thus Mary E. Outerbridge brought lawn tennis to America, and it was first played at the Staten Island Cricket Club in New York.

19. Cricket

CRICKET, of course, is another of the ball games that have slowly evolved from the ancient Egyptian-Arabian folk fertility rites. Scotland has claimed that it comes from their "Cat and Dog," at least so says Dr. Jamieson in his *Etymological Dictionary of the Scottish Language;* Pycroft suggests a fifteenth century "Handyn and Handoute," while others claim a very uncertain *Creag* of the fifteenth century as one of the many games played with club and ball from which cricket may have come.

Prior points out that *criquet* is the diminutive in medieval French of a word retained in all Germanic languages: Anglo-Saxon *cricc,* Danish *krykke,* German *Krücke,* Frisian *krik,* meaning a staff or crutch. Altham, the historian of cricket, notes that games usually take their name from the weapon, not the target, and that "in the mother tongue of the Aryan race there was a syllable beginning with *cr,* ending in a hard *c,* having its middle letter every variety of vowels according to tribal predilection, and meaning staff, or stick."

But the famous *New English Dictionary* favors a word used as a target: *criquet.* Du Cange quotes this word in a manuscript of 1478: "The suppliant came to a place where a game of ball (*jeu de boule*) was played, near to a stick (*attache*) or *criquet*," and defines *criquet* as "a stick which serves as a target in a ball game." Prior, however, doubts this definition: "I am strongly inclined," he says, "that in the first place it meant a "crook" and that cricket, like croquet, hockey, *la crosse* and *cambuc* (club) was once played with a bandy stick. Indeed *criquet* and *crocket* in English are, when traced back to their origin, merely developments of the Latin *crux*, as the two games are but developments of the same game." We may conclude, then, that the name *cricket* came from the Latin *crux* by way of one or more of the various European languages, and quite possibly through the French *criquet*. Prior makes another interesting observation, that the game of *jeu de boule* of Du Cange was "probably more like rounders than cricket," which supports the theory of the close relationship of cricket to circuit running games, of which stoolball was the earliest.

But where did the *game* come from? Altham answers, "Nothing except the generic club ball . . . Nor can we possibly point to a date when cricket ceased to be club ball and became itself." We can take this statement to be correct only with two provisos. First, if we understand by "club ball" not the name of a specific game, but a generic term for ball games played with some form of a club. Strutt invented this term in 1808, and his use of it has misguided historians into the belief that at one time there was an English ball game called "Club ball." So far there is no evidence that there was such a nomenclature in English for a ball game. Secondly, we must understand the nature of these club and ball games of the twelfth to fourteenth centuries. They were the descendants of the old French game of *la soule,* and further back, of the ancient Egyptian springtime fertility rites, not yet free from their folk customs and religious significance.

In certain places in the South of England these games, patterned by local customs and traditions, had taken the form of stoolball which we have already discussed. Andrew Lang and others have pointed out the relationship between stoolball and cricket, and Monckton heads a chapter "Cricket or stoolball," thus identifying as one the two games. Exception has been made to this theory on the ground that stoolball was "a somewhat delicate sister" of cricket, "evolved as a less strenuous variety of their brothers' sport by the country maidens, who used as a mark the familiar and obvious milking-stool." This objection to stoolball, far from ruling it out, tends to prove the case! Stoolball was associated with young maidens, also with springtime, and also with the Church. Stoolball was the time *par excellence* for country maids and their swains to do their courting: an obvious vestige of the ancient fertility rites associated with procreation.

Stoolball, we have seen, dates probably from 1330, but certainly from 1450, when John Myrc interpreted the Latin poem of William Pagula, written in 1330. A manuscript of 1344 in the Bodleian Library at Oxford (No. 264), shows a game of club and ball. One player throws the ball to another who holds a vicious-looking club. He defends a round object which resembles a stool but with a base instead of legs. A number of fielders stand behind the batter, with hands outstretched, ready to catch the ball. As played by our milkmaids, one player threw a ball at an upturned stool, its three legs in the air, defended by another player. In course of time a second stool was added, which obviously made a primitive form of cricket. Now a stool was also called a "cricket" and it is possible that the name cricket came from the three-legged stool, or that a similarity of sound combined with the French *criquet* hastened the adoption of the name. Nevertheless we have already voted in favor of the older etymology. Moreover, the earliest use of *cricket,* meaning a stool, was in 1643, while the earliest use of *cricket,* meaning the game, was in 1598, in Florio's Italian-English dictionary, *A World of Words.* There the word *sgrillare* is defined "to make a noise as a cricket; to play cricket-a-wicket." A reference in a manuscript in the Guildford Borough Records of 1598, quoted in most authorities, proves on later examination to be quoits and not cricket.

We claim, then, that cricket is a direct descendant of stoolball. But this statement is much too simple as it stands. Those who played stoolball were also familiar with forms of *jeu de la crosse* as played in Brittany and Normandy, and cricket was undoubtedly a synthesis of stoolball with the older French ball games. This theory is strengthened by illustrations of cricket which show that it was originally played with a curved stick, such as was used in *jeu de la crosse.* These appear both in England and in France. The illustration in the *Jeux des jeunes garçons* of 1810 pictures a very crude form of a club, and stones for wickets. "This game," says this source, "is little known in France. It is played only in certain provinces, where it is called *la crosse.* It resembles greatly the old *jeu de mail.*"

We may summarize: The game and name of cricket stem back to ancient games played with curved stick and ball, starting with *la soule,* and evolving in England through stoolball, but modified by *jeu de la crosse* and similar French ball customs.

20. Baseball: Infancy

IN THE chapter on stoolball we showed how a simple game played with upturned stools, an off-shot of more ancient customs, first made its appearance in the fourteenth century. It developed from a one base to a two base game, a progenitor of cricket, and then to games played with three, four and more bases. This game was first called stoolball but, as the number of bases increased, became known under other names, one of them "baseball."

The earliest mention of a game called baseball so far located was made by the Reverend Thomas Wilson, a Puritan divine at Maidstone, England. He wrote reminiscently in the year 1700, describing events that had taken place before that time, perhaps during his former years as a minister. "I have seen," he records with disapproval, "Morris-dancing, cudgel-playing, baseball and cricketts, and many other sports on the Lord's Day."

The next item on baseball is found in the year 1744 in an English book, *A Little Pretty Pocket-Book,* which we have already quoted on stoolball. It was published in London by John Newbery, one of the earliest publishers of children's books.

Modern Court Tennis court, Racquet and Tennis Club, New York.

Racquets Doubles Championship. England *vs.* America at the Racquet
and Tennis Club, New York, February, 1947. *Players are: K. A. Wagg,
F. F. de Rham, R. L. Gerry, Jr., I. Akers-Douglas.*

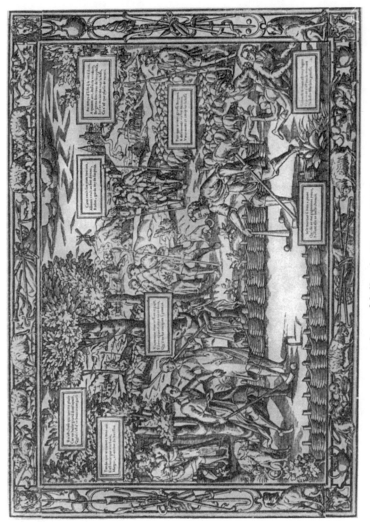

Ground billiards, France, 1460.

In the *Little Pretty Pocket-Book,* among other things designed to instruct painlessly the unsuspecting youth, were thirty pages of "alphabetically digested" games. Under each letter appeared a woodcut illustrating the game, a rhymed description of it and, last but not least, a *Moral.* One of the games presented was *Base-ball,* which was thus described:

BASE-BALL

The Ball *once struck off,*
Away flies the Boy
To the next destin'd Post,
And then Home with Joy.

Moral

Thus Britons for Lucre
Fly over the Main;
But, with Pleasure transported,
Return back again.

The woodcut illustrating the game shows three young players engaged in a game which is quite evidently a hit-the-ball base-running type of game. Three bases are marked by posts. At one a boy stands ready to strike the ball with his hand; at another post, first base, another player stands ready to run as soon as the batter strikes the ball, while a third player serves the ball. Although a base is called a *post* in the text of the poem, the name of the game is *Base-ball,* and the players must reach *Home.* It should be observed, however, that posts were used as bases until about 1860. Clearly this is a simplified form—an early fore-runner of the modern baseball.

The *Little Pretty Pocket-Book* passed through at least eleven English editions between the years 1744 and 1790. It was bound in an attractive gilt-flowered paper and was small enough to slip into a child's pocket. Undoubtedly it was quite popular with its young readers, who evidently wore out all copies of the first edition and all but a few copies of the later editions. No copy of the first edition seems to have survived —at least a long and careful search to locate a copy has been unsuccessful. We have used the Worcester, 1787 edition for our illustration, which is identical with the London 1767 edition. It may be assumed that there were no changes in the page under consideration in later editions.

The popularity of the *Little Pretty Pocket-Book* alone makes it evident that *Base-ball* was known to, and played by, English boys. That this is no assumption but a statement of fact is borne out by the testimony of Mary Lepell, who became Lady Hervey, noted for her "merit, beauty and vivacity" and celebrated in verse by Gay, Pope and Voltaire. In a letter dated November 14, 1748, Lady Hervey writes: "Tis really prodigious to see how deep the ladies play (at the gaming tables): but, in spite of all these irregularities, the Prince's family (i.e., the family of Frederick, Prince of Wales) is an example of innocent and cheerful amusements. All this last summer they played abroad; and now, in the winter, in a large room, they divert themselves at base-ball, a play all who are, or have been, schoolboys, are well acquainted with. The ladies, as well as the gentlemen, join in this amusement, and the latter return the compliment, in the evening, by playing for an hour at the old and innocent game of push-pin." And so it may be claimed that before 1750 a simple form of baseball was a popular children's game in England.

How and when did baseball come to America? That question can never be satisfactorily answered. It may have been brought by English children who crossed the Atlantic with their families. In all probability it did, but this, so far, cannot be proved. We do know it arrived in book form. It did not take long for the fame of Newbery's publications to reach America. Enterprising booksellers and printers soon recognized their merit and imported them in large quantities. In *The Pennsylvania Gazette* of November 15, 1750, a number of them are advertised.

By the year 1760 Hugh Gaine, a prominent New York printer, was importing practically all Newbery's books and in 1762 he pirated the first American edition of *A Little Pretty Pocket-Book*, with a slightly abbreviated title. This book, which was duly advertised in *The New York Mercury* of August 30, 1762, contained the first use of the term *base-ball* and the first illustration of the game printed in America. Unfortunately no copy of this edition can be found today, but there is still the possibility that some collector will be lucky enough to find it. Another edition, published in Philadelphia by W. Spotswood in 1786, is recorded but no copy has been found.

The American editions must have been popular for in 1787 *A Little Pretty Pocket-Book* was pirated a third time, this time by the famous New England printer, Isaiah Thomas of Worcester, Mass. His "First Worcester Edition" duplicated the English book even to its unusual gilt-flowered paper cover and faithfully reproduced, page by page, the English text and illustrations, but with certain exceptions. He Americanized it by substituting American equivalents whenever a phrase in the original sounded too English:

BASE-BALL

The Ball *once struck off,*
Away flies the Boy
To the next destin'd Post
And then Home with Joy.

Moral

Thus Seamen for Lucre
Fly over the Main,
But, with Pleasure transported
Return back again.

What may be the first record of an actual game of baseball played in America, and so called, is related in the *Journal* of a Revolutionary soldier, George Ewing who, at Valley Forge on April 7, 1778 "Exercisd in the afternoon in the intervals playd at base." Bat and ball games, we know, were played by American youngsters at this time and certainly they were known to Washington's men, for Ewing also records in his Journal that on two occasions they played cricket, or "wicket," as he called it.

There is strong evidence that the students of Princeton played at many forms of ball games, including baseball, before the end of the eighteenth century. Much of this is recorded in Varning Lansing Collins' *Princeton*. "The diary of 1786," says Collins, "contains several allusions to College sports—hockey on Stony Brook in winter, shinny, quoits, 'baste ball,' and 'prison baste' on the campus in the spring and summer." That 'baste ball' was baseball is supported by the further entry in the diary on March 22, 1786: "A fine day, play baste ball in the campus but am beaten for I miss both catching and striking the ball." What may be a further mention of baseball is a prohibition by the College authorities: "It appearing that a play at present much practised by the smaller boys among the students and by the grammar Scholars with balls and sticks in the back common of the College is in itself low and unbecoming gentlemen Students, and in as much as it is an exercise attended with great danger to the health by sudden and alternate heats and colds and as it tends by accidents almost unavoidable in that play to disfiguring and maiming those who are engaged in it for whose health and safety as well as improvement in Study as far as depends on our exertion we are accountable to their Parents & liable to be severely blamed for them: and in as much as there are many amusements both more honourable and more useful in which they are indulged, Therefore the faculty think it incumbent on them to prohibit both the Students & grammar Scholars from using the play aforesaid."

Jesse Holliman, in his *American Sports (1785-1835)* mentions other cases of ball games played in the period of the infancy of baseball. One of the correspondents of the Baseball Commission which made its famous report in 1907, Mr. George H. Stoddard, former postmaster and a leading citizen of Upton, Mass., stated that the game of Round Ball was played by his father in the year 1820 "and he has the tradition from his parent that two generations before, directly after the Revolution, it was played and was not a novelty even then. Round Ball was, in fact, the game of the period." *Round Ball* was one of the names under which the game now called *baseball* was then known.

The eighteenth century, then, might be called the period of the infancy of baseball. The game was known in both England and America under various names, one of which was baseball. But it was played in primitive form, for apparently no definite rules had yet been formulated. The game was traditional in that it was handed down by word of mouth, or practical demonstration, from generation to generation. Primarily it was a game for boys, although adults were known to indulge in the game occasionally.

21. Baseball: Adolescence

THE period between 1800 and 1840 may be called the adolescence of baseball, for although during these years the popularity of boys' bat-and-ball games increased tremendously in England, America and France, they had not yet attained maturity. The dawn of a new era for children was breaking and it was no longer considered to be wicked to indulge in innocent pastimes. But it was a tough battle and those who had the temerity to promote healthful pastimes for youth had continually to pander to those who were responsible for their moral welfare. It was rare to find a book of games without an accompaniment of morals and maxims, and physical development was always impressed upon the innocent youngsters as being of very slight importance compared with their spiritual well-being.

A fine example of the sort of thing boys and girls had to endure is to be found in *The Instructor and Guide for Little Masters*. Cricket, this book said, was "a manly exercise! But full of admonition. It is only fit for athletic or strong constitutions. It requires great labour, and constant quick motion of the body; and causes a profusion of sweat in proportion. The secret pleasure in this exercise is to prove yourself a better man than your antagonist. But take care that you do not over-play your part; and instead of excelling work your ruin and destruction. What will it avail in such a contest to say I have conquered Will or Tom with the loss of my life! or with a broken constitution!

"Neither let it be a temptation to grow up with you. Let it be ever so agreeable to constitution, or take ever so much pleasure in batts and balls, let it not interfere with the duties of a man's life. Recreation is not sinful, is not forbidden by the laws of God or nations, except it divert a man from his business by which he is to live, or consumes his substance or fortune, which he holds in trust from Providence to promote his own interest in life, to support his credit, and to provide for those committed to his care."

No doubt these are all worthy sentiments, but it must have been irksome to those early nineteenth century boys, when struggling to get the rules of a game, to have to wade through such moral teaching.

The idea of exercise in the open as a health measure was slowly making headway. As early as 1659 the great educator Comenius had advocated indoor and out of door games as healthful exercise, and mentioned the game of tennis in par-ticular, but it took a hundred and fifty years for the idea to get across to the popular mind. Soon after the year 1800 we find a sudden spurt in the development of out of door games, and this bat-and-ball base-running game seemed to become the most popular of all.

One of the most interesting pieces of evidence for this period is a fascinating little book of boys' games, *Les jeux des jeunes garçons, représentés par vingt quatre estampes, accom-*

pagnés de l'explication détaillée des régles, d'anecdotes his-toriques . . . . , published in Paris about the year 1810. This book is noted as the fourth edition, but unfortunately we have not yet been able to locate earlier editions, which were probably issued between 1800 and 1810. We do not know what may be in the earlier editions, but this 1810 edition contains a game called *La balle empoisonnée,* or *Poisoned Ball.* Two games are grouped under the one title of poisoned ball, both of which have as a major characteristic the rule that a player is "out" when touched with the ball, just as he is in modern baseball.

One form of poisoned ball is described thus: "Eight or ten children divide themselves into two teams. In a court, or in a large square space four points are marked: one for the home base, the others for bases which must be touched by the run-ners in succession. Lots are drawn; the winning side occupies the home base. (That is the entire side stands in the batter's box.) The others place themselves about the four bases at distances which they judge to be suitable. One of their team pitches to one of the players in the home base. He strikes the pitched ball, and runs to first base, to second, and to others in turn if there is time for it. Another player strikes the ball in turn, and makes first base while his comrade makes second, and so on, but two players on the batting-team may not oc-cupy the same base.

"The fielding team must field the ball as promptly as possi-ble, in order to touch one of the runners before he reaches base. If a player is touched by 'the poisoned ball' (before he reaches base) he stops, and his team (is out). The team leaves home base, and must serve the ball in turn. But if the player (who is struck with the ball), or one of his team, is able to field the ball quickly, and strike one of the opposing team with it before he reaches home base (then the incoming team is out, and the first team remains at bat). If a batter is careless enough to strike it in such a way as to allow one of the fielders to catch it before it touches the ground, then his side (is out, and) must leave the batter's box.

"The game provides good exercise in a large court, in which the four corners form the bases. In an open place the bases may be made with the coats (of the players). But it is inconvenient to have to run too far to field the ball, and the team at bat is apt to have too long an innings."

This game is clearly a fore-runner of baseball. Where did the compiler of this French book get it? Did the game develop in France from ancient games, as poisoned ball, while a similar game, after being introduced from France, developed in England as base-ball? We do not wish to rob France of her just claims as the mother of bat and ball games: cricket and baseball undoubtedly stem from French beginnings. But this nineteenth century French compiler, we venture the opinion, got his material from English sources: the more mature game recrossed from England back to France. The game of cricket is described in the book; the second form of poisoned ball is identical with the English game of nine holes, or hat ball, included in contemporary English books. Poisoned ball is none other than the English game of base-ball, or rounders as it was called at this time. It is still played in France, as are other similar games, such as *La balle au camp* and *La balle chasseur*. Early in the nineteenth century a similar game known as *Ball-Stock* was played in Germany. The presence of so many English games in this book leads to the conclusion that the compiler drew on English sources for his information. It

141

is possible that earlier English rules will be found, but in the meantime *Les Jeux des Jeunes Garçons* holds the distinction of being the first book, so far located, to contain the printed rules of a bat-and-ball base-running game.

The French youngsters evidently took to the game as healthy boys anywhere would. In the year 1822 another edition of *Les Jeux des Jeunes Garçons* repeated the rules of the game, added historical notes which mentioned ball games of the North American Indians and, as was the custom of the day, introduced a little moral poem. 'Poisoned ball' was compared to the poisoned word: slander. Such a practical application in a later edition of the book surely implies that in the author's mind the game was familiar enough to the youngsters for whom the book was intended. Here is a rough translation of the poem:

POISONED BALL (BASEBALL)

My dear Justin, why do you spread
False rumours about a fellow playmate?
Your heart, without doubt, is far from sharing
This wrong, the result of a momentary pique.
Get wise to yourself. Harbour such thoughts no longer,
And get into a game and banish that ill temper.
So spake a wise teacher.
Monsieur Justin, the slanderer,
Run to Robert, make friends, and on the advice of a teacher,
Suggest a game in which many others may take part.
Ten or twelve youngsters form two teams,
    Get into a game of baseball
    To see the day come to a happy ending.
Of four bases, marked by the coats
    Of all our heedless youngsters,
    One is selected.
That is the home base: to occupy it is great joy.
    After his ill humour has passed,

Although Justin does not deserve it,
The choice is decided in his favour.
Robert pitches; he warms up, serves the ball.
Soon comes Justin's turn:
With all his might, after his strike,
He scampers towards the three other bases.
Suddenly he is hit. Instead of a long lecture
The teacher then speaks in his ear:
Just as this ball
Stopped you as you ran,
And made your team mates
Bawl you out in good style,
As they wrathfully left
The batter's box—
This ball is, my dear child,
The symbol of slander.

Mother of Despair, and daughter of Envy,
Scourge of society,
This monster is ever detested.
In school and city it poisons life,
And too often, at its first step,
Stops an honest man, or a man of ability,
Just when, by their endeavour, they are about to make home base.
M. AUGUSTE.

The period of adolescence of baseball in England is marked by an increasing interest in the game. As it was played from place to place, slight changes in the rules were made and the game given different names in different localities. The name *base-ball* still lingered. Jane Austen called it *base-ball*. In her *Northanger Abbey*, which was published in 1818 although written in 1798, we read: "Mrs. Morland was a very good woman, and wished to see her children everything they ought to be; but her time was so much occupied . . . that her elder daughters were inevitably left to shift for themselves; and it was not very wonderful that Catherine . . . should prefer cricket, base-ball, riding on horseback, and running about the country, at the age of fourteen, to books."

There is a most interesting list of games played in the county of Suffolk in Edward Moor's *Suffolk Words and Phrases* which was published in the year 1823. "We have (in Suffolk)," said Moor, "and no doubt so have other counties, a great variety of amusing games, active and sedentary . . . Omitting games so universal as Cricket, Leap-frog, Marbles, etc., we have All the birds in the air, and All the fishes in the sea—Bandy, Bandy-wicket, Base-ball, Bandy-ball, Bubble hole . . . Foot ball, Hocky, Nine holes . . ." and so on through a long list of names. In London about this time the game was called *Feeder*. But gradually the name of *Rounders* came to the fore, and it was under this name that the first rules were printed. The name of *Rounders* has persisted to this day in England.

In the year 1828 a compilation of boys' games was published in London, called *The Boy's Own Book: a complete encyclopedia of all the diversions, athletic, scientific and recreative.* It was published by Vizetelly, Branston and Co., and the dedication reads: "To the Youth of Great Britain, This Volume, Compiled expressly for their Instruction & Amusement is Dedicated, With the Best Wishes of the Publishers." Its compiler was William Clarke, who in this book produced the best compilation of childhood games that had yet been made. Its success was immediate: three thousand copies were sold without advertising of any kind in little more than two months; it ran through seven editions by 1832, twenty by 1849, and netted the publishers £600 a year for many years. Second and third editions, put quickly on the market, contained many "alterations and improvements" one of which was the inclusion of the game of rounders. Possibly the game appeared in the second edition of 1828 or 1829, but since no copy of this can be found, this is uncertain. It is in the third London edition of 1829.

In the 1829 edition of *The Boy's Own Book* appeared for the first time in English, so far as can be determined at the present time, a set of rules for any of the popular base-running games. The fact that the name "rounders" was selected, instead of the earlier name "base-ball," indicates that the former name was in more general use about the year 1829. That the sale of the book was so steady also testifies to the popularity of the games described in it, and we may assume that rounders, as a boys' game, was well established in England by that time.

Perhaps a brief description of the game of rounders will help the reader. Two sides are picked. Usually there is no set number on a side, this being governed by the number of players available, but at one time the number on a side was limited to eleven. The entire side at bat stands in a large batter's box, the other side being in the field, as at baseball. A soft ball is used. A bat is sometimes used, but the ball may be struck with the hand if bats are not available. The pitcher serves and the runners make bases exactly as they do in baseball. In some places if a batter strikes at and misses three balls he is out. But in others, he is allowed to wait until he is served a "good" ball. If a runner is struck by a thrown ball (not touched with it as in baseball) while between bases, he is out. The batsmen circulate around the bases, as in baseball, gradually losing men who have been put out, until no one is left in the batter's box. When this occurs the side is out and the opposing side has its innings. If a batter is caught out in rounders, not only he but his whole team is out. When it is time to change innings the team in the field must rush to the batter's box as quickly as possible, for on the instant a team is out one of their players may seize the ball, throw it at an opposing player, and so put him out. In the account of the game as played in France, previously described, this procedure put the whole team out, but in the English rounders just one man at a time could be put out. If a "home run" is scored, or a "rounder" as it is called, a man who has been put out returns to his team. There is no set number of innings, the teams taking turn at bat as long as they choose to play. Of course there are variations and, just as an American group of boys will revert to One Old Cat, and so on, when the players are not numerous enough to form sides, so will English boys fix up substitute games to suit the number of players.

In America the period of adolescence was much more striking than in England. The old game of baseball was making considerable headway, but here too, for lack of written rules, there was no uniformity. On the contrary, just as it had done in England, the game varied with locality, and its name changed from place to place. Sometimes it was called Town Ball, or Round Ball, even Goal Ball, for bases were also known as goals. But "baseball" was the favorite name and "baseball" finally won out. All over New England, between the years 1800 and 1840, games were played, mostly by young boys, but gradually by young men at college and university, and even by grown men.

Thurlow Weed, for instance, in his *Autobiography* tells how as a young man at Rochester, N. Y., in the year 1825, he was a member of a flourishing baseball club: "Though an industrious and busy place, its (Rochester's) citizens found leisure for rational and healthy recreation. A base-ball club, numbering nearly fifty members, met every afternoon during the ball playing season. Though the members of the Club embraced persons between eighteen and forty, it attracted the young and the old. The ball ground, containing some eight or ten acres, known as Mumford's meadow, by the side of the river, above the falls, is now a compact part of the city. Our best players were Addison Gardiner, Frederick Whittlesey, Samuel L. Selden, Thomas Kempshall, James K. Livingston, Dr. George Marvin, Dr. F. F. Backus, Dr. A. G. Smith, and others."

Baseball was a most popular pastime at Brown University as early as 1827. Williams Latham, who attended Brown from 1823 to 1827 noted in his diary on March 22, 1827: "We had a great play at ball today noon." If the Baseball Hall of Fame is looking for the first "fan," here he is, for while there are many earlier references to baseball, Latham is the first to show enthusiasm. "We this morning . . . ," his diary records on Monday, April 9, 1827, "have been playing ball, But I never have received so much pleasure from it here as I have in Bridgewater. They do not have more than 6 or 7 on a side, so that a great deal of time is spent in running after the ball, Neither do they throw so fair ball. They are afraid the fellow in the middle will hit it with his bat-stick." Did the Brown students limit the number on a side? Latham complained that they did, but there is no record that they set a definite number. And to Brown University goes the distinction, if we might call it that, to be the first to "walk" a batter when he was known to be in the Babe Ruth class, or at least a primitive version of the art of avoiding a heavy hitter.

Dr. Franklin Bonney in a memoir of General Fighting Joe

147

Hooker, of Civil War fame, which appeared in the Springfield (Mass.) *Republican* of May 8, 1895, speaks of Hooker's enthusiasm for baseball as a boy, which would be about the year 1830. "The meanwhile," Bonney says, "he enjoyed and was active in all boyish sports. At baseball, then a very different game from now, he was very expert; catching was his forte. He would take a ball from almost in front of the bat, so eager, active and dexterous were his movements."

A game very closely resembling baseball or rounders, played by Indians early in the nineteenth century, is described in a little book, *Female Robinson Crusoe*, published in New York in the year 1837. "Some of the male adults were playing ball, which article was . . . portion of a sturgeon's head, which is elastic, covered with a piece of dressed deerskin. Another ball . . . was constituted of narrow strips of deerskin, wound around itself, like a ball of our twine, and then covered with a sufficiently broad piece of the same material.

"In playing this game they showed great dexterity, and swiftness of speed. The party engaged, occupied an extensive surface of open ground, over whose whole space a vigorous blow with the hickory club of the striker would send the ball, and also to an amazing height. On its coming down, it was almost invariably caught by another player at a distance, and as instantly hurled from his hand to touch, if possible, the striker of the ball, who would then drop his club, and run, to a small pile of stones, which it was part of the game for him to reach. If the runner succeeded in reaching to the desired spot, before the ball touched him, he was safe. Otherwise he had to resign his club to the fortunate thrower of the ball against him, and take his place to catch. The run-

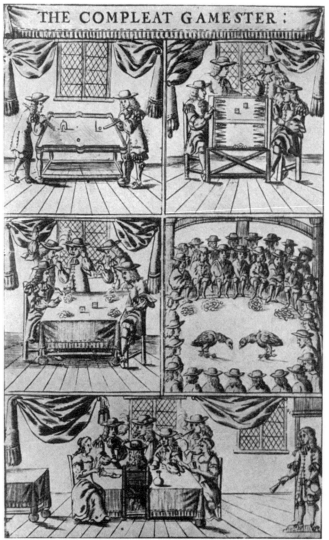

THE COMPLEAT GAMESTER:

Billiards played with "port" and "king," 1674.

Louis XIV playing billiards, *by A. Trouvain.*

Hurling, England, 17th Century.

ner, by watching the coming ball, was almost always enabled to avoid its contact with him, by dodging or leaping . . . If that was effected, another person, in his own division of the playing party (there being two rival divisions), assumed the dropped club, to become striker in his turn.

"Their principal object seemed to be, to send the ball as far as possible, in order to enable the striker of it, to run around the great space of ground, which was comprised within the area formed by piles of stones, placed at intervals along the line of the imaginary circle."

This book purports to be the narrative of one, Lucy Ford, who endured a long and solitary residence in the Western Wilderness. It must, however, be classed as fiction and the game described discounted as "Indian." But it does disclose a person, the unknown author, with a knowledge of the game of baseball in the year 1837.

Testimony that the game of baseball was not confined to New England but was general throughout the United States in the year 1831 is to be found in a little book by Horatio Smith, first published in 1831 and later in 1832, 1833 and 1836, called *Festivals, games and amusements*. "The games and amusements of New England," said Smith, "are similar to those of other sections of the United States. The young men are expert in a variety of games at ball—such as cricket, base, cat, football, trap ball . . ."

In a press release, before it made its final decision, the Spalding Baseball Commission quoted letters from several correspondents who gave instances of games before 1830: "Timothy Tait, now living in Worcester (i.e. in 1906), aged 97, played Round Ball as early as 1822 . . . J. A. Mendum of 591 Dudley Street, Dorchester, Mass., who is now eighty three years old, states that . . . in 1830, he, with other pupils of the grammar school in School Street, Portsmouth, N. H., played the genuine game of base ball regularly during the summer, on Wednesday and Saturday afternoons . . . Mr. Stoddard says: 'Four Old Cat and Three Old Cat were as well known to Massachusetts boys as was Round Ball. My father played them between 1800 and 1820. The games then bore the same relation to Rounders that 'scrub' now bears to baseball. If the boys assembled and found that there were not enough on hand to make up a team of Round Ball, they would content themselves with Four Old Cat or Three Old Cat." Here we have evidence that rounders was known in the United States by 1820.

When Col. Jas. Lee was made an honorary member of the old Knickerbocker Club in 1846, he claimed that he had played baseball as a boy, which would have been about the year 1800. So popular was "ball-playing" in the streets of Worcester, Mass., in 1816, that the city fathers passed an ordinance forbidding it. Dr. Oliver Wendell Holmes in his later years said that he played baseball at Harvard, and he graduated in 1829. "Mr. Charles Bost, the catcher and captain of the Knickerbockers, played baseball on Long Island fifty years ago, (i.e. in 1838) and it was the same game the Knickerbockers afterward played."

In 1910 Andrew H. Caughey wrote to the New York *Tribune:* "I am in my eighty-third year, and I know that seventy years ago (i.e., in 1840), as a boy at school in a country school district in Erie County, Pa., I played Base Ball with my schoolmates; and I know it was a common game long before my time. It had just the same form as the Base Ball of today, and the rules of the game were nearly the same as they are now. One bad feature of the old game, I am glad to say, is not now permitted. The catchers, both the one behind the batter and those on the field, could throw the ball and hit the runner between the bases with all the swiftness he could put into it—'burn him,' it was called." It will be noted that this "Base Ball" which Caughey played was similar to both rounders and town ball, in that a base-runner could be put out by "soaking" him with the ball as he ran. This was characteristic of all base-running games prior to 1840.

A charming little woodcut showing a group of boys "Playing Ball" appeared in *Children's Amusements*, published by Samuel Wood in 1820, and again in his *New York Primer* of 1823. The side having its innings—three boys—stands in the batter's box. One boy pitches, the batter is striking the ball, and one base-runner runs in a clockwise direction, as was customary in the early days. Here is a simple boyhood game.

But well before 1840 at least one form of the game was customarily played by adults. This was Town Ball, so called, because it used to be played at the time the Town Meetings were held. A town ball team was fully organized in Philadelphia in 1833 and it continued to be played in New England until 1860, where it was known as "The Massachusetts Game." Town ball varied from baseball or rounders in that the batter's box was midway between two bases, making a kind of fifth base. The bases were wooden stakes, four and a half feet high. The "home" plate was the fourth base. A base-runner did not make a complete circuit. It closely resembled rounders in that the batter could wait until he judged that he had a good pitch at which to strike, and he could be put out by being struck with the ball between bases.

Thus we see copious evidence of early forms of baseball

played in the United States before the year 1829. But still no printed rules existed and there was no criterion by which rules could be made uniform in different parts of the country.

The publication of *The Boy's Own Book* in England, in 1829, was quickly followed by its publication in America: in the same year it was published in Boston. It was a tremendous contrast to the juvenile books of the period, which emphasized piety, morals and instruction of mind and soul; it must have been received with whoops of delight by the youngsters of both countries. Its success in England had been immediate and its reception in America was acclaimed by pedagogue and pupil.

"This beautiful work," said a book review in *The Classical Journal and Scholars' Review*, of Boston, "fully corresponds with its title, being emphatically a perfect encyclopedia of sports and pastimes congenial to youth, either in summer or in winter; abroad, in the fields; or at home, by the social fireside, and conducive equally to the formation of a healthy frame (it was too polite to say 'body'), by the practice of the athletic sports; and to habits of correct thinking, by the illustration of a great variety of ingenious and scientific problems and amusements . . . Its republication in this country does credit to the liberality and discrimination of the publishers; and we are well satisfied that the present edition is fully equal, in point of interest, to the English copy."

At least one eminent American has gone on record as to the influence of this book in his boyhood days. Edward Everett Hale, when a boy, had but six books: Scott's minor poems, *Scientific Dialogues, Harry and Lucy, The Treasury of Knowledge, Robinson Crusoe* and, as he put it, "One hesitates before he writes so great a name, *THE BOY'S OWN*

BOOK. Now let me speak," he continues, "with bated breath, of the dear *Boy's Own Book.* If I had seen Nansen before he started, I would have asked him to look at the North Pole to see if there were a copy there, for I cannot find a copy anywhere now in the world . . . My copy, I suppose, has long since fed the eagles and the condors, and apparently nothing is left of it but these loving impressions which it has made on grateful memory. Who made the *Boy's Own Book* I do not know, and I wish I did; I would write his grandson the most grateful letter that he ever received. . . . It told about checkers and chess and magic lanterns. It told about fencing and swimming and riding and walking . . . It was whispered that in the English edition there were chapters which were left out in the American edition; and one day Edward Webster brought round the English edition, to our astonishment. But little did we heed this; there was more in the American edition than we could digest with our limited resources . . . Let me hope that the boys of to-day have books half as good; I am sure that they have none better."

No wonder this little book inspired Edward Everett Hale to such raptures! It must have been a Godsend to hundreds of boys. To it all American boys owe a tremendous debt of gratitude for, when it reprinted the rules of the game of rounders, it was the first germination of the seed of the game of baseball that had lain dormant in American soil for over fifty years. It crystallized the unformulated rules of the many base-running games, made a definite game out of them and started the pastime that was to become America's national game.

"In the west of England," *The Boy's Own Book* records, rounders "is one of the most favourite sports with the bat and ball. In the metropolis, boys play a game very similar to it,

153

called Feeder." A diamond-shaped field is shown typograph- ically: technically this may not be a "diagram," but it is the first indication of a diamond used in a bat-and-ball game in America. The pitcher, then known as a "pecker" or "feeder," is shown in an appropriate place by the letter *e,* while the catcher is "the one who stands behind *a,*" the home plate. The distance between bases varied according to the size of the field available for play. The batter (striker) is out "if he miss three times": here is the origin of the three-strikes-out rule. One "foul" is out, although it is not so called. When the batter strikes the ball he "drops the bat, and runs" just as he does today. In the old game, as in the modern, the players have the same nostalgic attraction for "home." In this game of rounders as described the players ran clockwise instead of counter-clockwise, as in the modern game. A batter was out if the ball were caught, but he was also out if struck by a thrown ball while running between bases. Evidently the game con- sisted of one inning a side, unless, as may be implied, the sides rotated as long as they pleased. The texts of the Boston, 1829, and London, 1829, editions are identical except for two typographical errors: "posts" became "pots" and "out-play- ers" became "players."

As was common in those days imitators were quick to "bor- row" a good idea and in 1834 the firm of Lilly, Wait, Colman, and Holden, of Boston, published a book of games called *The Book of Sports,* by Robin Carver. "I have been indebted," said Carver in the Preface, "to the English edition of *The Boy's Own Book,* the price of which work places it beyond the reach of most young people of this country." It reprinted many of the games in the English book but—and this should be noted well—when it came to the game of rounders the old heading of "Rounders" was changed to "Base, or Goal Ball." "This game," said Carver, "is known under a variety of names. It is sometimes called 'round ball,' but I believe that 'base' or 'goal ball' are the names generally adopted in our country." This book marks an epoch in the history of baseball in America for here we have the first printing of the rules of baseball, called by that name. The game of baseball in Robin Carver's *Book of Sports* is merely the game of rounders with a substitute heading.

Baseball on Boston Common, 1834.

The description of the game of baseball in Carver's *Book of Sports* of 1834 varies little from the rules for rounders as given in *The Boy's Own Book* of 1829. The introductory paragraph, referring to the places in England where the game was played, is omitted. A few abbreviations and slight

155

changes in the text are made. The one-foul-out rule is omitted, but the method of putting out a base-runner by striking him with the ball is retained. A comparison of the two books can leave no doubt that here we have the transition of the English game of rounders into the American game of baseball.

The Boy's Own Book	The Book of Sports
BY WILLIAM CLARKE	BY ROBIN CARVER
London, 1829	Boston, 1834
ROUNDERS	BASE, OR GOAL BALL

In the west of England this is one of the most favourite sports with the bat and ball. In the metropolis, boys play a game very similar to it, called Feeder. In rounders, the players divide into two equal parties, and chance decides which shall have

c   first innings. Four stones
     or posts are placed from
b d twelve to twenty yards
     asunder, as *a*, *b*, *c*, *d*, in
e   the margin; another is
a   put at *e*; one of the
     party which is out, who
is called the pecker or feeder, places himself at *e*. He tosses the ball gently toward *a*, on the right of which one of the in party places himself, and strikes the ball, if possible, with his bat. If he miss three times, or if the ball, when struck, fall behind *a*, or be caught by any of the out players, who are all scattered about the field except one who stands behind *a*, he is out, and another takes his place. If none

This game is known under a variety of names. It is sometimes called 'round ball,' but I believe that 'base', or 'goal ball' are the names generally adopted in our country. The players divide into two equal parties, and chance decides which shall have

c   first innings. Four stones
     or stakes are placed
b d from twelve to twenty
     yards asunder, as *a*, *b*,
e   *c*, *d*, in the margin;
a   another is put at *e*. One
     of the party, who is out,
places himself at *e*. He tosses the ball gently toward *a*, on the right of which one of the *in-party* places himself, and strikes the ball, if possible, with his bat. If he miss three times, or if the ball, when struck, be caught by any of the players of the opposite side, who are scattered about the field, he is out, and another takes his place. If none of these accidents take place, on striking the ball he drops

Golf, Flemish, 1560.

Baseball in France, 1810. (Poisoned ball.)

Lacrosse in Canada, 1875.

of these events take place, on striking the ball he drops the bat, and runs toward *b*, or, if he can, to *c, d*, or even to *a* again. If, however, the feeder, or any of the out players who may happen to have the ball, strike him with it in his progress from *a* to *b*, *b* to *c*, *c* to *d*, or *d* to *a*, he is out. Supposing he can only get to *b*, one of his partners takes the bat, and strikes at the ball in turn; while the ball is passing from the feeder to *a*, if it be missed, or after it is struck, the first player gets to the next or a further goal, if possible, without being struck. If he can only get to *c*, or *d*, the second runs to *b* only, or *c*, as the case may be, and a third player begins; as they get home, that is, to *a*, they play at the ball in rotation, until they all get out; then, of course, the out players take their places.

the bat, and runs toward *b*, or, if he can, to *c, d*, or even to *a* again. If, however, the boy who stands at *e*, or any of the out-players who may happen to have the ball, strike him with it in his progress from *a* to *b*, *b* to *c*, *c* to *d*, or *d* to *a*, he is out. Supposing he can only get to *b*, one of his partners takes the bat, and strikes at the ball in turn. If the first player can only get to *c*, or *d*, the second runs to *b*, only, or *c*, as the case may be, and a third player begins; as they get home, that is, to *a*, they play at the ball by turns, until they all get out. Then, of course, the out-players take their places.

Carver's *Book of Sports* makes one other bid for fame. Not only did it print the first rules of baseball in the United States, but it also printed the first real American illustration of the game. The *Little Pretty Pocket Book* was earlier, but it merely reprinted an English picture. The earlier woodcut of Samuel Wood, undoubtedly a primitive form of baseball, was called "Playing Ball," not "Baseball." Robin Carver gave us an illustration of an American game played, of all places, on Boston Common! What could be more American than that? Although Carver's book does not say so, there can be no doubt as to the location of the game in the picture. The matter is clinched by an advertisement in T. G. Fessenden's

Complete Farmer and Rural Economist, published by Lilly, Wait and Company in 1834, which reproduces the illustration with the caption "Scene on Boston Common." Moreover, the use of the intersecting paths on the Common as part of a diamond suggests that from this practice arose the idea of marking the diamond on the turf. Yes, the publication of Robin Carver's *Book of Sports* in 1834 was a most important event in baseball history.

The following year, in 1835, the illustration from Carver's *The Book of Sports* was reprinted in a little child's book of moral instruction entitled *The first lie; or, Falsehood its own punishment.* Baseball was not mentioned in the book, and the illustration bore the caption: *The Playground of Mr. Watt's School.* We do not know if this school was adjacent to the Boston Common, but there can be no doubt as to the scene, for the State Capitol rising majestically in the background settles the matter.

Again in 1835 the firm of Cory and Daniels, of Providence, R. I., published a little paper-backed juvenile, *Boy's and Girl's Book of Sports, Embellished with Cuts,* which drew on the popular *Boy's Own Book* of 1829, and reprinted the rules for rounders, substituting the heading "Base, or Goal Ball." Two editions of *The Boy's and Girl's Book of Sports* appeared before 1839: the first in 1835 and the second in 1836. Two later editions are known, that of 1843, and the latest published about the year 1860. In all copies examined the game Base, or Goal Ball appears with but slight changes.

The second definite step in the march of baseball was taken in the year 1839 when *The Boy's Book of Sports: a description of the exercises and pastimes of youth* was published by S. Babcock in New Haven. This little book was a much more intelligent compilation than its predecessors. The publisher frankly acknowledged the source of his information, *The Boy's Own Book,* "a beautiful London work," but revised the text to fit in with the experience of American boys:

GAMES AT BALL

"The ball is a favorite toy, not only for those for whom our little book is designed, but often with 'children of a larger growth.' The number of games played with it is very great, but the limits of our book will only allow us to describe some of the most common.

" 'Base ball' is played by a number, who are divided into two parties, by the leader in each choosing one from among the players alternately. The leaders then toss up for the innings. Four stones for goals are then placed so as to form the four points of a diamond, as seen in the margin. The party who are

*   out, then take their places (*see picture*), one stands
2   4   near the center of the diamond, to toss the ball for
3   one of the in-party who stands with his bat at *.

Another stands behind the striker to catch the ball, if he fail to hit it. A third stands still farther behind, to return the ball when necessary. The remainder are dispersed about the field, to catch the ball when knocked, or to return it if not caught. If the striker miss the ball three times, or if he knock it and any of the opposite party catch it, he is out, and another of his party takes his place; if none of these accidents happen, then, on striking the ball, he drops his bat and runs to 2, or, if the ball be still at some distance, to 3, or 4, or even back to *, according to the circumstances; but he must be cautious how he ventures too far at a time, for if any of the opposite party hit him with the ball while he is passing from one goal to another, he is out. When the first has struck the ball, another takes the bat, and strikes, and runs in like manner; then a third, and so on through the party, and as they arrive at *one after another, each, who are not out, take their turns again, until all are out. Then, of course, the other party takes their places."

This book marks a distinct development of the game of baseball *via* the rounders route. The name of the game starts with "Rounders," then to "Base, or Goal Ball" and finally to "Base Ball." The rules are concise and intelligent: obviously written by someone who had played the game. The numbering of the bases differs slightly from modern practice, being called Home, second, third and fourth bases. In these rules, for the first time, the players are instructed to run in a counter-clockwise direction, as is done today. The cut illustrating the game of baseball in *The Boy's Book of Sports* of 1839 was a reprint of the picture of Boston Common in Robin Carver's *Book of Sports* of 1834.

This New Haven publication of 1839 marks the end of the period of adolescence of baseball in the United States. The amorphous games of the earlier days, played without uniformity in many places, crystallized when the rules were at last put down in print. Having been set down in print it was natural that successive printings, taking advantage of the experience of boys and young men throughout the country, should show gradual revision and improvement. By 1840 the game had "grown up."

22. Baseball Attains Maturity

THURLOW WEED has recorded that he was a member of a baseball club as early as the year 1825 in Rochester, N. Y., but that club made no permanent contribution to the game, and soon passed into obscurity.

Henry Chadwick, writing in 1860, said that a baseball club called the New York Club played in New York City "before the Knickerbockers," which would place it about the year 1840. But the credit for bringing the game of baseball into a robust maturity belongs to The Knickerbocker Base Ball Club of New York City.

In the year 1842 a number of New York gentlemen used to gather for "health, recreation and social enjoyment." They were men of standing in the community, physicians, brokers, successful merchants: leaders of the business life of the city. They were wont to gather on a plot of ground at the corner of Twenty-Seventh Street and Madison Avenue on sunny days, in search of outdoor exercise, which took the form of the primitive ball games of the time. It was customary for two or three of them to round up enough players to make a match. Before very long the march of the growing city made it necessary for them to move "up-town" to the Murray Hill section, "between the railroad cut and Third Avenue."

Some of the names of the members of this group of gentlemen have been preserved: they included Col. James Lee, Dr. Ransom, Abraham Tucker, James Fisher, W. Vail, Charles H. Birney, Dr. Daniel I. Adams, Fraley C. Nichols, Charles S. DeBost, Henry T. Anthony and Alexander J. Cartwright. In the spring of 1845, after three years of unorganized play had elapsed, Alexander J. Cartwright, "one day upon the field proposed a regular organization, promising to obtain several recruits." This statement is made on the authority of the early historian of the game, Charles A. Peverelly. Since Cartwright undoubtedly was one of the leaders of the new organization, it can be taken as correct. To Alexander J. Cartwright, therefore, goes the credit as the prime mover in the organization of The Knickerbocker Base Ball Club of New York, from which all modern baseball has grown.

A committee to organize the proposed club was appointed, consisting of W. R. Wheaton, Alexander J. Cartwright, D. F. Curry, E. R. Dupignac, Jr., and W. H. Tucker. Soon enough names were obtained and a preliminary meeting was held. It was suggested that, as it was apparent they would soon be driven from Murray Hill, some suitable place should be obtained in New Jersey, where their stay could be permanent. A few days later the players assembled, crossed over the Barclay Street ferry and, after scouting around for a while, selected the Elysian Fields at Hoboken, where they settled.

Where did the Knickerbockers get their game of baseball? What rules did they play from 1842, when they first met, until late in 1845, when they issued their famous rules? D. F. Curry related that on one afternoon when the group was at play a Mr. Wadsworth presented for consideration a diagram of a baseball field laid out substantially as it is today. "The plan caused a great deal of talk," said Mr. Curry, "but finally we agreed to try it." Some writers have shrouded this diagram of Wadsworth in a great deal of mystery. There is no direct evidence that the Knickerbockers consulted any printed book of rules when they formulated their own, but the great popularity of Carver's *Book of Sports, The Boy's Own Book, Boy's and Girl's Book of Sports,* and *The Boy's Book of Sports,* which totaled several editions, and must have run into hundreds if not thousands of copies before 1842, must have resulted in the knowledge of a "diamond-shaped" field for a base-running game in the minds of hundreds of boys. In fact, as we have shown, boys all over the country played these games. There need be no mystery about the genesis of the Knickerbocker rules. They came directly or indirectly from these popular books of boys' games.

At any rate, on September 23, 1845, after what must have been a highly interesting summer during which they experimented with the proposed rules, The Knickerbocker Base Ball Club was organized and at the same time a set of rules to govern their play was adopted. The first officers of the Club were: Duncan F. Curry, President; Wm. R. Wheaton, Vice-President and William H. Tucker, Secretary and Treasurer. The rules of the Club were also the rules of the game. Here they are:

RULES OF THE KNICKERBOCKER BASE BALL CLUB
Adopted September 23, 1845

1st. Members must strictly observe the time agreed upon for exercise, and be punctual in their attendance.

2d. When assembled for exercise, the President, or in his absence, the Vice-President, shall appoint an

Umpire, who shall keep the game in a book provided for that purpose, and note all violations of the By-Laws and Rules during the time of exercise.

3d. The presiding officer shall designate two members as Captains, who shall retire and make the match to be played, observing at the same time that the players put opposite to each other should be as nearly equal as possible; the choice of sides to be then tossed for, and the *first in hand* (i.e., the first at bat) to be decided in like manner.

4th. The bases shall be from "home" to second base, forty-two paces equidistant.

5th. No stump match shall be played on a regular day of exercise.

6th. If there should not be sufficient number of members of the Club present at the time agreed upon to commence exercise, gentlemen not members may be chosen in to make up the match, which *shall not be broken up* to take in members that may afterwards appear; but, in all cases, members shall have the preference, when present, at the making of a match.

7th. If members appear after the game is commenced they may be chosen in if mutually agreed upon.

8. The game to consist of twenty-one counts, or aces; but at the conclusion an equal number of hands must be played. (That is, the team scoring twenty-one runs first wins, but each side must have the same number of players at bat before the game is ended.)

9th. The ball must be pitched, and not thrown for the bat, (that is, the ball must be served underhand with unbent elbow, and not thrown as is done today).

10th. A ball knocked out of the field, or outside the range of the first or third base, is foul.

11th. Three balls being struck at and missed and the last one caught is a hand out; if not caught is considered fair, and the striker bound to run.

12th. If a ball be struck, or tipped, and caught, either flying, or on the first bound, it is a hand out.

13th. A player running the bases shall be out, if the ball is in the hands of an adversary on the base, or if the runner is touched with it before he makes his base; it being understood, however, that in no instance is a ball to be thrown at him.

14th. A player running who shall prevent an adversary from catching or getting the ball before making his base, is a hand out.

15th. Three hands out, all out.

16th. Players must take their strike in regular turn.

17th. All disputes and differences relative to the game, to be decided by the Umpire, from which there is no appeal.

18th. No ace or base can be made on a foul strike.

19th. A runner cannot be put out in making one base, when a balk is made by the pitcher.

20th. But one base allowed when a ball bounds out of the field when struck.

> WILLIAM R. WHEATON,
> WILLIAM H. TUCKER,
> *Committee on By-Laws.*

The founding of the Knickerbocker Club marks the beginning of organized baseball. But it should be emphasized that the Knickerbocker Club was strictly amateur, and that its original purpose was not so much to play baseball, as to provide a group of gentlemen with a means of exercise, and an opportunity for social amenities. The first rule, for instance, talks of the time "agreed upon for exercise," and the second rule likewise speaks of the time when the members "assembled for exercise."

Nor was the Knickerbocker Club the first of its kind. Much earlier, as we have seen about the year 1800, a group of men belonging to the leading families in New York, feeling the need of some healthy game for exercise, selected the game of racquets, united in a rather informal organization, took over a building to which a racquets court was attached and began what is now the Racquet and Tennis Club of New York.

Rule number two of the Knickerbocker Club provided that the Umpire of each game should record the score in a special book. Perhaps it is to this rule that the Club owed its influence and its success. The original "Game Book" may still be seen in the New York Public Library, with each game carefully and neatly recorded. The making of a match in those days was attended with most punctilious etiquette. Formal invitations had to be in writing, duly laid before the Club and formally accepted. For instance, here is a request for a game from the Empire Base Ball Club:

New York, Aug. 12, 1856

To the Officers and Members
  of the Knickerbocker Base Ball Club.
Gentlemen:
  At the Regular Monthly Meeting of the Empire Base Ball Club held on Monday evening, 11th inst., the following resolution was offered and adopted by the Club, viz.: "That an invitation be extended to the Knickerbocker Club to play a friendly game of Ball, the said game to take place at their earliest convenience, also that no Collation will be given."

Yours respectfully,
THOS. CHALMERS, JR.,
Secretary of
Empire Base Ball Club.

Any communication may be addressed to
  Thos. Chalmers, Jr.
  203 Pearl Street.

Yes, indeed, the Knickerbockers were an exclusive set: their club was strictly limited to men of their own choosing, and to be selected for a game with them was a privilege extended to but few of the other baseball clubs which rapidly organized to play the game. When an invitation was accepted it usually meant a dinner, or at least a "collation" afterwards; the match became a social occasion. It must have been with some temerity that the Empire Base Ball Club suggested the omission of the collation.

The Knickerbocker rules were a tremendous advance over the old rules in the children's books such as the *Boy's Book of Sports* of 1839, but they were still far from the rules of the game as played today. A game was completed when one side scored twenty-one runs; it might be finished in one inning or might go on indefinitely. The first game played between the Knickerbockers and another team, the New York Club, consisted of four innings only. The New York Club, possibly because it was the older organization and its members therefore better skilled in the game, won by 23 to 1. This was on June 19, 1846, at the Elysian Fields, Hoboken. The Umpire must have had a tough time, he was forced to fine one of the New York players, Davis by name, six cents for swearing! We hereby nominate Davis for baseball's Hall of Fame!

A rule that caused some difficulty was that which declared a batter out if his strike was caught on the first bound. The Knickerbockers liked this rule and stuck to it when they played among themselves. But, as more teams developed, there was less liking for the out-on-first-bound regulation, so that when matches were arranged the letters would stipulate that the games would be "on the fly" or, simply, "fly games." This meant that the out-on-bound rule would not be observed and that the ball must be caught "on the fly," before it touched the ground. The Knickerbockers faced severe opposition in regard to this rule and they discussed it hotly in their own meetings. Finally they capitulated and, at a Special Meeting of the Club held to discuss the matter, they passed a resolution to abolish it.

Wherever athletic games have been played there have always been two groups of followers: those who were interested in the game for the game's sake, the real sportsmen, and those whose interest lay in methods of exploiting the skill of others, the gamblers and the professionals. As organized baseball spread it became impossible to maintain the high standards of amateurism as set by the Knickerbockers and they disbanded in 1882.

With the Knickerbockers, baseball made a flying start. As interest developed and time passed, new rules were introduced, until we have the finished product as it is known today. Its subsequent history has already been told: it is not the purpose of this book to repeat it, but only to show how the game started.

Let us summarize: Back in ancient times there was the Egyptian-Arabic fertility rite; this crossed to Europe in the ninth century and was converted into an Easter Christian ritual some time after 1000 A.D. The Christian rite became secularized into the game of *la soule* and similar ball customs and slowly spread, dividing into local variations, one of which was the fourteenth century game of stoolball in England. As bases were added to the one originally used in stoolball it became known as baseball as early as 1700, and under a variety of names, such as rounders and feeder, before 1800. Then a period of adolescence from 1800 to 1840 in both England and America, when base-running games spread rapidly, again under different names. At last the rules appeared in the French *Jeux des Jeunes Garçons* of 1810, as "poisoned ball," and then in English in *The Boy's Own Book* of 1829, as "Rounders." We have seen how the rules of this game of rounders were adopted in America as baseball and then, step by step, through Robin Carver's *Book of Sports* of 1834, to culminate in the *Rules* of the Knickerbocker Base Ball Club of 1845. Thus the game of baseball as played in America today is the descendant, remotely, of the older English game of "base-ball" and, directly, of the English game of rounders.

23. *The Doubleday-Cooperstown Myth*

MANY Americans today have been led to believe that baseball was invented by Abner Doubleday at Cooperstown, N. Y., in the year 1839. As recently as 1905 no one had associated the name of the famous Civil War General with the game. When the claim was made that baseball was a purely American game, the idea that it was devised by a patriot and a soldier appealed to the popular imagination; no questions were asked and the theory accepted as a proper and fitting solution to a long-standing mystery. How did this theory originate, and what basis is there for the claim?

Although the first baseball club, The Knickerbockers of New York, was organized in the year 1845, it was not until after the Civil War that the game became really popular. Then, of course, the curious wondered from whence it came and the unanimous answer, as recorded in the handbooks of the period, was that both baseball and the earlier game of Town Ball were developments of the "old English game of rounders." Such books as C. A. Peverelly's *The Book of American Pastimes,* published in 1866, made no bones about the matter but bluntly declared that baseball was a descendant of the English rounders.

But, as the popularity of the game spread, enthusiasts began to look on baseball as an "American" game, as opposed to the "English" games of cricket and rounders. Patriotic emotion became confused with sportsmanship; rounders as an origin of baseball was indignantly denied and the game claimed as an entirely American pastime, with its roots nowhere but in American soil.

In the 1880's feeling ran high; it reached its peak in James Montgomery Ward's *Base-ball: how to become a player*, published in 1888. Ward's defense of the American origin and his scorn for those who suggested English sources was vehement in the extreme. "The assertion," he said, "that baseball is descended from rounders is a pure assumption, unsupported even by proof that the latter antedates the former, and unjustified by any line of reasoning based upon the likeness of the games."

But still, in spite of the lack of supporting evidence—and it is curious that until 1937 no such documentary evidence was produced—the theory lingered. One of the strongest supporters of the rounders theory was the gentle "Father of Baseball" himself, Henry Chadwick. But Chadwick, although he did more than any other man in the early days to build up the game of baseball into America's national game, happened to have been born in England. As long as opinions could not be supported by facts, he was ruled out as one too biased to render an impartial judgment on the subject.

On the other hand, Albert G. Spalding, the well-known player and sporting goods dealer, warmly defended the American theory. Spalding, as Francis C. Richter says, was "superlatively great as player, manager, club owner and in business as it related to Base Ball. He was the greatest propagandist

171

and missionary the game ever knew and spent more time, labor and money in spreading the gospel of Base Ball than any other man of record."

Although Spalding and Chadwick were warm personal friends, they failed to convince one another as to the origin of the game which played so large a part in their lives. Many a time they discussed the matter and many a time they aired their views in print. At last Spalding decided to settle the matter once and for all and in his *Official Base Ball Guide* for 1905 he sought to bring things to a head.

"There seems to be a conflict of opinion" wrote he, "as to the origin of Base Ball. I think the game has arrived at an age and at a point in its development when the mooted question should be settled in some comprehensive and authoritative way, and for all time.

"Some authorities, notably Mr. Henry Chadwick, claim that Base Ball is of English origin and was a direct descendant of the old English juvenile pastime called "Rounders," while others claim that it was entirely of American origin, and had nothing whatever to do with Rounders or any other foreign game.

"While I concede that Mr. Chadwick's Rounder theory is entitled to much weight because of his long connection with Base Ball and the magnificent work he had done in the upbuilding of the game for upwards of fifty years, yet I am unwilling longer to accept his Rounder theory without something more convincing than his oft-repeated assertion that 'Base Ball did originate from Rounders.'

"For the purpose of settling this question I hereby challenge the Grand Old Man of Base Ball to produce his proofs and demonstrate in some tangible way, if he can, that our national game derived its origin from Rounders.

"Mr. Chadwick, who, by the way, is of English birth, and was rocked in a "Rounders" cradle, says in support of his theory that 'there is but one field game now in vogue on this continent which is strictly American in its origin, and that one is the old Indian game of Lacrosse, now known as the Canadian national game. Base Ball originated from the old English schoolboy game of Rounders, as plainly shown by the fact that the basic principle of both games is the field use of a bat, a ball and bases.'

"I have been fed on this kind of 'Rounders pap' for upwards of forty years, and I refuse to swallow any more of it without substantial proof sauce of it."

Thus challenged A. G. Spalding in 1905 and, to settle the matter, he suggested a Commission to study the matter, and to arrive at a definite conclusion. There is something amusing in the way that Spalding assumed that a point of history could be "settled in some comprehensive and authoritative way, *for all time.*" No historian is bold enough to say that his research has been thorough enough, all inclusive enough, to settle any matter without any possibility that the disclosure of further evidence in the future, may modify or upset his findings. Unfortunately there are many points which are not susceptible to such an easy solution: the origin of baseball is one of them. It should not be forgotten in this connection that A. G. Spalding was the head of a large and prosperous sporting goods concern that still bears his name. He would not be averse to any incidental publicity which might accrue to his firm in the unraveling of the mystery of baseball. Was the publicity his major interest?

173

Six public-spirited men, all well known and all associated
with baseball, accepted honorary positions on the Spalding
Baseball Commission. They were: A. G. Mills, of New York,
an enthusiastic ball player before and during the Civil War,
and the third President of the National League. The Hon.
Arthur P. Gorman, Senator from Maryland, who died before
the Commission rendered its decision. The Hon. Morgan G.
Bulkeley, at one time Governor, and at that time United
States Senator from Connecticut. He was first President of
the National League. N. E. Young, of Washington, D. C., a
veteran ball player, the first Secretary and afterwards the
fourth President of the National League. Alfred J. Reach, of
Philadelphia, head of a sporting goods house, known as the
"Business Genius of Base Ball." George Wright of Boston, a
former player of note and later a leading business man in
sport.

Mr. James E. Sullivan, of New York, President of the Amateur Athletic Union, accepted the position as Secretary of the
Commission and it got under way in the year 1905 by inviting all and sundry to send in whatever information they had.
The work of collecting and checking this material fell upon
Mr. Sullivan; during the next two years a mass of correspondence from writers all over the country came to his office. From
time to time Sullivan would send out scraps of information to
the press, inviting others to send in whatever they knew of
the early history of the game.

At last, in December, 1907, A. G. Mills issued the report of
the Commission which, he said, "should forever set at rest the
question as to the Origin of Base Ball." Again that sublime air
of authority! It is amazing how anyone could issue such a
ridiculous statement. The Commission itself seems to have

174

done little work. Its report consists of three letters: one from Henry Chadwick, summarizing the rounders theory; one from A. G. Spalding, in which he attempted to summarize evidence submitted to the Commission in support of the American theory; and one from James Montgomery Ward, supporting Spalding's contention.

Chadwick claimed that "the established national American game of Base Ball had for its origin the old English schoolboy game of 'Rounders,' and this latter game existed in England as far as two centuries ago; and, in fact, it is a question at issue in England as to whether 'Rounders' did not antedate the time-honored game of Cricket itself." But Chadwick produced no documentary evidence to substantiate his case. He based his entire argument on the fact that the basic principle of both games was the same: "two opposing sides of contestants, on a special field of play, in which a ball was pitched or tossed to an opposing batsman, who endeavoured to strike the ball out into the field, far enough to admit of his safety running the round of the bases, so as to enable him to score a run, to count in the game—the side scoring the most runs winning the game—fully identifies the similarity of the two games." The impartial student must admit that Chadwick did not give facts to prove his case. It was an expression of opinion only.

Spalding in his brief began by claiming "that the game of Base Ball is entirely of American origin, and has no relation to, or connection with, any game of any other country," although he did admit that "all games of ball have a certain similarity and family relationship." His opening sentence contains two contradictory statements. What he said, in effect, was "Base Ball . . . has no relation to . . . any game of any other country, except . . . family relationship!" Not a very good start.

He charged that the general impression in the public mind that Rounders was the source of baseball had been "occasioned largely, if not entirely, by the very able base ball writings of my esteemed and venerable friend, Mr. Henry Chadwick, who for the past 40 years has continued to make the assertion that Base Ball had its origin in Rounders. If Mr. Chadwick had been born in this country," continued Spalding, "he might be as totally ignorant of rounders as the rest of us, but it so happened that before he came to this country, when he was about 10 years of age, he had seen or probably played in a game of rounders, but I do not recall that he claims to have ever seen or played a game of rounders since his arrival in America."

Spalding stated what might be called his simplified history of baseball. First the old colonial game of One Old Cat, which was played by three boys; then Two Old Cat, played by four boys; then Three Old Cat, played by six boys and, finally, Four Old Cat, played by eight boys. Then, according to Spalding, "some ingenious American boy" figured out how to "change the individual players . . . into competing teams," and so developed Town Ball. The trouble with this outline is that it is much too simple—and is not in accord with historical fact.

The high spot of the Spalding evidence was the testimony submitted by Abner Graves, a mining engineer of Denver, Colo., who was the first to make the claim that Abner Doubleday invented baseball in Cooperstown, N. Y., in the year 1839. "In this connection," wrote Spalding, "it is of interest to know that this Abner Doubleday was a graduate of West Point in

1842, and afterward became famous in the Civil War as the man who sighted the first gun fired from Fort Sumter, April 12, 1861, which opened the War of the Rebellion between the North and the South. He afterward became a Major General in the United States Army and retired from service in 1873, and died January 26, 1893.

"Mr. Abner Graves was a boy playmate and fellow pupil of Abner Doubleday at Green's Select School in Cooperstown, N. Y., in 1839. Mr. Graves, who is still living (1907), says he was present when Doubleday first outlined with a stick in the dirt the present diamond-shaped Base Ball field, including the location of the players in the field, and afterward saw him make a diagram of the field on paper, with a crude pencil memorandum of the rules for his new game, which he named 'Base Ball.' As Mr. Graves was one of the youths that took part in this new game under Doubleday's direction his interesting and positive account is certainly entitled to serious consideration."

On the testimony of Abner Graves, with no other supporting evidence, Spalding claimed that:

1. Baseball was invented by Abner Doubleday.
2. The place of invention was Cooperstown, N. Y.
3. The date of invention was 1839.
4. The game was named "Base Ball" by Doubleday.
5. The diamond-shaped field was invented by Doubleday.
6. The locations of the players on the field were first designated by Doubleday.
7. When Doubleday for the first-time marked out a diamond, the event was witnessed by Abner Graves.
8. Doubleday immediately thereafter put down on paper the rules of the game, and a diagram of the field.

It should be noted that no mention was made in the Spalding letter of the limitation of the number of players on a side, and no mention of the method of putting a player out.

"Personally," said Spalding, "I confess that I am very much impressed with the straightforward, positive and apparently accurate manner in which Mr. Graves writes his narrative, and the circumstantial evidence with which he surrounds it, and I am strongly inclined to the belief that Major General Abner Doubleday was the originator of the game. It certainly appeals to an American's pride to have had the great national game of Base Ball created and named by a Major General in the United States Army." The patriotic approach made a telling appeal to the judges, but it had no bearing on the facts one way or another.

James Montgomery Ward's letter strongly supported the American origin of baseball, in spite of the fact that he stated that "all exact information upon the origin of Base Ball must, in the very nature of things, be unobtainable." His testimony, like Chadwick's, remains a matter of opinion, unsupported by fact. He made no mention of Doubleday.

On December 30, 1907, A. G. Mills, as President of the Special Base Ball Commission, made his report, which was undersigned by Morgan G. Bulkeley, Nicholas E. Young, A. J. Reach and Geo. Wright. Mills paid his compliments to Henry Chadwick, but respectfully disagreed with his opinion. "Surely there can be no question of the fact that Edison, Frank Sprague and other pioneers in the electrical field were the inventors of useful devices and processes whereby electricity was harnessed for the use of man, although they did not invent electricity, nor do they, nor does anybody, know today what electricity is! As I understand it, the invention or the origination of anything practical or useful, whether it be in the domain of mechanics or field sports, is the creation of the device or process from pre-existing materials or elements; and, in this sense, I do not, myself, see how there can be any question that the game of Base Ball originated in the United States and not in England—where it certainly had never been played, in however crude a form, and was strange and unfamiliar when an American ball team first played it here."

The Mills report proceeded to speak at length of Doubleday's military record, and particularly of the fact that Mills and Doubleday belonged to the same military post in the G.A.R. Mills served on the guard of honor when Doubleday's body lay in state, on January 30, 1893, in the New York City Hall, prior to its interment in Arlington. "I can well understand," Mills wrote, "how the orderly mind of the embryo West Pointer would devise a scheme for limiting the contestants on each side and allotting them to field positions, each with a certain amount of territory; also substituting the existing method of putting out the base runner for the old one of 'plugging' him with the ball." This is an excellent example of what is called "begging the question." Moreover, a further claim is added, that Doubleday substituted the present method of touching a base-runner with the ball, instead of the older method of throwing the ball at him. Just where Mills got this idea is difficult to say. It was not in the Graves' letter and, as will be shown later: it is not true.

Doubleday, it was claimed, had made the original diagram of the diamond-shaped field in 1839. The Knickerbocker Club had played baseball in New York City in 1842, and organized in 1845. Was it possible to show a connection between the two events? If Doubleday invented the game, there must

179

have been continuity between the two events. "I am also much interested," continued Mills, "in the statement made by Mr. Curry, of the pioneer Knickerbocker Club, and confirmed by Mr. Tassle, of the famous old Atlantic Club of Brooklyn, that a diagram, showing the ball field laid out substantially as it is today, was brought to the field one afternoon by a Mr. Wadsworth. Mr. Curry says 'the plan caused a great deal of talk, but finally we agreed to try it . . .' It is possible that a connection more or less direct can be traced between the diagram drawn by Doubleday in 1839 and that presented to the Knickerbocker Club by Wadsworth in 1845, or thereabouts, and I wrote several days ago for data bearing on this point, but *as yet it has not come to hand.*"

With this summation, Mills came to the following "deductions from the testimony submitted":

First: That "Base Ball" had its origin in the United States.

Second: That the first scheme for playing it, according to the best evidence obtainable to date, was devised by Abner Doubleday at Cooperstown, N. Y., in 1839.

The decision of the Commission was hailed by A. G. Spalding as a great victory and as a decision that settled once and forever the great question of baseball's origin. He publicized it in his book *America's National Game,* which was published in 1911, and for twenty-five years the decision remained unquestioned. Text-book writers, sporting writers, historians, seemingly fascinated by the august set-up of the Commission, swallowed uncritically the verdict. Or was it a hesitancy to disturb what has become one of America's most popular traditions?

Only one voice was raised in objection to the report of the Commission and its decision on the Cooperstown-Doubleday origin, that of Will Irwin in *Collier's Magazine* of May 8, 1909. But the protest went unheeded.

Tradition or no tradition, the facts must be examined and given due consideration, whenever research discloses any new evidence.

24. The Myth Exploded

A SURVEY of the material upon which the Spalding Baseball Commission based its decision leaves one amazed and incredulous that such an important matter should have been decided on such meagre affirmative evidence and in the face of so much evidence which belied its findings.

Unfortunately the vast correspondence handled by the Secretary of the Commission, James E. Sullivan, was burned in the fire at The American Sports Publishing Company, Warren Street, New York City, in the year 1911. It is impossible to check the original data, including the original letter from Abner Graves containing his testimony on Doubleday. One of the most important records remaining is a press release, issued by Sullivan, or someone associated with him, which is now in the collection of papers of A. G. Mills at the New York Public Library. Quotations have already been made from this document, showing that several people testified as to various forms of baseball long before Doubleday, notably Timothy Tait, J. A. Mendum and G. H. Stoddard. The game of Town Ball was well known to Spalding and Ward and their letters to the Commission told in detail of this early American ball game. All references to these forerunners of baseball were utterly disregarded and a decision arrived at on the basis of one solitary document without any supporting evidence of any kind.

Why did the Commission make such a decision? There can be but one explanation. They were all men of integrity, public spirited and held positions of honor. But they were busy men. They evidently assumed that their positions on the Commission were "honorary," that is, that someone else would do the work. It is extremely doubtful if any member of the Commission except A. G. Mills, the Chairman, saw anything of the evidence submitted. They merely read the report submitted to them by the Chairman for their approval. After marking time for almost three years, they were urged to settle the matter. Albert Goodwill Spalding was a forceful personality, and one who had spent the best years of his life in the game. If he expressed an opinion in no uncertain terms, what could the Commission do but, out of deference to the leader in the world of baseball, gracefully decide in his favor? This they did. The decision was a courteous gesture to Spalding, a kind of recognition of his place as a leader in the sporting fraternity.

How much evidence is there to support the conclusion that baseball was invented by Doubleday at Cooperstown, N. Y., in 1839, and that therefore the game "had its origin in the United States"? The letter of Abner Graves to the Spalding Commission, and nothing else. Not a single piece of evidence has ever been found to support the claim. The letter was not directly quoted by Spalding, but may be found in the press release of the Spalding Commission mentioned above. It reads as follows:

"The American game of base ball was invented by Abner Doubleday of Cooperstown, N. Y., either the spring prior or following the 'Log Cabin and Hard Cider' campaign of General William H. Harrison for the presidency. Doubleday was then a boy pupil of Green's Select School in Cooperstown, and the same, as General Doubleday, won honor at the battle of Gettysburg in the Civil War. The pupils of Otsego Academy and of Green's Select School were then playing the old game of Town Ball in the following manner:

"A 'tosser' stood close to the 'home goal' and tossed the ball straight upward about six feet for the batsman to strike at on its fall, the latter using a four-inch flat-board bat. All others wanting to play were scattered about the field, far and near, to catch the ball when hit. The lucky catcher took his innings at the bat. When a batsman struck the ball he ran for a goal fifty feet distant and returned. If the ball was not caught or if he was not 'plunked' by a thrown ball, while running, he retained his innings, as in Old Cat.

"Doubleday then improved Town Ball, to limit the number of players, as many were hurt in collisions. From twenty to fifty boys took part in the game I have described. He also designed the game to be played by definite teams or side. Doubleday called the game 'Base Ball', for there were four bases to it. Three were places where the runner could rest free from being put out, provided he kept his foot on the flat stone base. The pitcher stood in a six foot ring. There were eleven players on a side. The ball had a rubber center over-wound with yarn to a size somewhat larger than the present day sphere, and was covered with leather or buckskin. Anyone getting the ball was entitled to throw it at a runner between the bases and put him out by hitting him with it.

"I well remember some of the best players of sixty years ago. They were Abner Doubleday, Elihu Phinney, Nels C. Brewer, John C. Graves, Joseph Chaffee,

John Starkweather, John Doubleday, Tom Bingham
and others who played at the Otsego Academy campus;
although a favorite place was on the 'Phinney Farm',
on the west shore of Otsego Lake."

What appears to be another letter from Abner Graves appears in Ralph Birdsall's *The Story of Cooperstown,* which
was published at Cooperstown in 1918, and again in 1920.
"Abner Doubleday," reads this letter, "was several years older
than I. In 1838, or 1839, I was attending the 'Frog Hollow'
school south of the Presbyterian Church, while he was at
school somewhere on the hill. I do not know, neither is it
possible for anyone to know, on what spot the first game was
played according to Doubleday's plan. He went diligently
among the boys of the town, and in several schools, explaining the plan, and inducing them to play Base Ball in lieu of
other games. Doubleday's game was played in a good many
places around town: sometimes in the old militia muster lot,
or training ground, a couple of hundred yards southeasterly
from the Court House, where the County Fairs were occasionally held; sometimes in Bennett's field south of Otsego
Academy; at other times over in Miller's Bay neighborhood,
and up the lake.

"I remember one dandy fine, rollicking game where men
and boys from the Academy and other schools played up on
the Phinney's farm, a mile or two up the west side of the
lake, when Abner Doubleday and Prof. Green chose sides,
and Doubleday's side beat Green's badly. Doubleday was
captain and catcher for his side and I think John Graves and
Elihu Phinney were the pitchers for the two sides. I wasn't
in the game, but stood close by Doubleday, and wanted
Prof. Green to win. In his first time at bat Prof. Green missed

three consecutive balls. Abner caught all three, then pounded
Mr. Green on the back with the ball, while they and all others
were roaring with laughter, and yelling 'Prof. is out!' "

Let us compare these letters with the testimony as submitted by Spalding, and upon which the commission based
its decision.

The date of the "invention" of baseball by Doubleday is
set by Spalding at 1839, on the letter of Graves, which said:
"either the spring prior or following the 'Log Cabin and Hard
Cider' campaign of General Harrison." Actually, this would
have been 1839 or 1840. As a matter of fact, Doubleday was
not in Cooperstown in 1839 or 1840. He entered West Point
Military Academy on September 1st, 1838, and was not in
Cooperstown on leave or otherwise in 1839 or 1840. In Graves'
letter to Birdsall he gave the date 1838 or 1839.

This variation in dates is one of the characteristics of the
Graves' letters which demonstrates how hazy was his recollection. He was equally hazy as to Doubleday's schooling.
In the earlier letter Doubleday was said to have been a pupil
of Green's Select School; in the later letter he went "to school
somewhere on the hill."

"Mr. Graves," according to Spalding, "says that he was
present when Doubleday first outlined with a stick in the dirt
the present diamond-shaped Base Ball field." There is no such
statement in the original Graves' letter. On the contrary
Graves clearly stated, "I do not know, nor is it possible for
anyone to know, on what spot the first game was played according to Doubleday's plan." Thus the "first" game of baseball, so dramatically featured by Spalding, and the traditional
authority for what is now Doubleday Field at Cooperstown,
N. Y., existed nowhere but in the fertile imagination of

Spalding. This "first" game is repudiated by Graves himself.

Spalding then claimed that at this historic "first" game, which existed so vividly in his imagination, Doubleday indicated "the position of the players on the field, and afterward saw him make a diagram of the field on paper, with a crude pencil memorandum of the rules of his new game, which he called Base Ball." The Graves letter does say that Doubleday called the game "Base Ball," but he makes no mention of a "diagram of the field," nor of the "crude pencil diagram of the rules."

Incredible? Yes, but that is not all. Neither Spalding, nor Ward in his letter, and certainly not Chadwick, made any reference to the change in putting out a base-runner from the old method of throwing the ball at a runner, to the present method of touching him with it. Yet, in his summation of the evidence, A. G. Mills claimed that this change had been made by Doubleday: "I can well understand," said he, "how the orderly mind of the embryo West Pointer would devise a scheme for limiting the number of contestants on each side, and allotting them to field positions, each with a certain amount of territory; also substituting the existing method of putting out the base runner for the old one of 'plugging' him with the ball."

Again we say incredible! Here is the Chairman, sitting as an impartial judge to weigh the evidence laid before the Commission, inserting in his summation material not to be found in the evidence at all! "I can well understand," he said (a better word would have been *imagine*) "how Doubleday would" (not *did*) "substitute the existing method of putting out a player." Where did Mills get this idea? This is one of

187

the big points of the Doubledayites, yet Spalding made no such claim on Doubleday's behalf, while Graves specifically belied it. In his original letter to the Commission he remarked: "Anyone getting the ball was entitled to throw it at a runner between the bases and put him out by hitting him with it."

Graves' evidence was that of an old man given *sixty-eight years after the events involved.* We have already noted some inconsistencies in his testimony. How many men over eighty years of age can accurately describe specific events of their boyhood days? Graves recollected that he played baseball. Hundreds of other men might have given similar testimony for, as we have seen, it was played in one form or another under more than one name, all over the United States long before Doubleday. Doubleday may have *played* baseball, as did hundreds of his contemporaries, but he did not *invent* it! That idea germinated in the senile brain of the ancient Abner Graves. Possibly Doubleday was a natural leader among his boyhood chums and possibly baseball, or rounders, was one of his favorite games. Graves, groping dimly into his youthful experiences, seized upon one of the outstanding members of his group, a boy some years older than himself and perhaps an object of "hero worship" and sixty-eight years later thrust upon him a fame to which he was no more entitled than any other boy of his time.

For Abner Doubleday did have fame thrust upon him—at least as far as baseball is concerned. There is no record that he made any personal claim to be its inventor. No contemporary records exist connecting him with the game. His obituary in the *New York Times* of January 28, 1893 makes no mention of baseball, nor does the memorial volume published

La Sueca, as played by Indians in Chili, 1712.

Jeu de la crosse, 18th century Brittany.

Ancient Maya Ball Court at Chichen Itza, Yucatan.

by the New York State Monuments Commission in 1918. In a letter recalling his youth he made no mention of baseball. "In my outdoor sports," he says, "I was addicted to topographical work, and even as a boy amused myself by making maps of the country."

A recognition of Doubleday as the originator of baseball may seem to be implied by the presence in the guard of honor, when his body lay in state at New York City Hall, on January 30th, 1893, of A. G. Mills of New York. Mills had been an enthusiastic ball player before and after the Civil War, and became third president of the National League.

Actually no such recognition was intended. By a coincidence Mills happened to be a member of the same veteran military organization as Doubleday, and was Commander of the Grand Army Post (Lafayette) at the time of the ceremonies. Doubleday's name was in no way associated with baseball until the press release of the Commission, already quoted, which was issued some time before June, 1906.

What, then, is Doubleday's contribution to baseball? Nothing, according to "the best evidence obtainable to date." He did not invent the *name:* it existed as early as 1700 in England and was in popular use in the United States before 1830.

He did not invent the *game:* the evidence clearly indicates its transition from the game of rounders and the existence of printed rules as early as 1834.

Doubleday did not devise the "diamond:" the diamond-shaped field is indicated in the illustration and rules of *Les Jeux des Jeunes Garçons,* of 1810 and 1822, the *Boy's Own Book* of 1829, and the word's first use in print, in connection with baseball, in the 1838 *Boy's Book of Sports.*

189

He did not originate the team system, as opposed to the rotation of players, as the earlier rules show.

It is claimed that Doubleday limited the number of players to eleven on a side, but this was an old rounders rule.

The claim that Doubleday substituted the existing method of putting out a base runner by touching him with the ball, instead of "soaking" him with the ball as he ran, we have shown to be false.

One more claim on behalf of Doubleday has been made: that he was the first to allot fielding positions. But this was gratuitously placed into the Commission's report, with no testimony to warrant it. It was a figment of the imagination of A. G. Mills.

According to Graves there is no justification for the selection of Doubleday Field at Cooperstown, N. Y. as the birthplace of baseball.

Nor is there any justification for the claim that Doubleday drew up a set of rules. Outside of the imaginative brain of Spalding they never existed: no one ever saw them—certainly not Abner Graves, the foundation upon which the Doubleday legend was erected.

If any American town should suddenly find itself in the limelight because of the discovery of an important historical event within its borders, it would be natural for the citizens of that town to make the most of such discovery. To fitly commemorate historical events is manifestly right and proper in any locality.

Unfortunately, in this commercial age, there is always the tendency to exploit any advantage of historical association. One can understand local pride, which may vary in magnitude with the importance of the event commemorated, and can allow a modest reward to those whose duty it is to care for the ancient shrines. But when such activities mount into the realm of business, and private gain displaces reverence and devotion, the public is not slow to sense the difference.

At Cooperstown the exercises at the time of the Baseball Centennial reached huge proportions. If the Cooperstown claims had been perfectly legitimate their heavy exploitation might have been tolerated. But what can be said of a situation in which, to quote *The New York Times,* "The canny sports writer now refers to Abner with his tongue thrust firmly in his cheek?" Since the Doubleday-Cooperstown story is now acknowledged to be, as *The Sun* of New York calls it, "a popular and harmless legend," any attempt to continue it as such becomes highly questionable.

When the report of the Spalding Baseball Commission was made in the year 1907 the surprised citizens of Cooperstown hailed their good fortune with delight. Indeed, what village or town in the country would not be glad to be revealed as the birthplace of baseball? And so they set about to make proper recognition of the fact.

The decision of the commission, reads a Cooperstown circular, "was accepted in sports circles throughout the country. The State of New York gave its official sanction by erecting a marker at the entrance to Doubleday Field which embraces the original playground of these schoolboys and is located in the heart of the historic village of Cooperstown.

"This movement progressed in a modest manner for several years. Subscriptions towards the purchase of the property were solicited by a committee of which the late Dr. E. L. Pitcher was chairman, under the auspices of the Cooperstown Chamber of Commerce. The plot was leased by the vil-

191

lage authorities to be used as a public playground, June 2, 1919, and in this manner the cradle of baseball first came into the possession of the public.

"September 6, 1920, Doubleday Field was formally opened with a baseball game between two local teams, President John A. Heydler of the National Baseball League was present and umpired the first inning, and one of the official umpires of the National League completed the game.

"On the date this opening took place the movement to purchase the site had advanced to a point where it was possible to announce that subscriptions to the amount of $3,019 were on hand. Three years later the taxpayers at a special election authorized the purchase of Doubleday Field and appropriated the funds necessary to complete the purchase. Title to the property was officially transferred to the Village of Cooperstown by a Supreme Court order dated September 29, 1923.

"The property leading from Doubleday Field to Main Street, providing a spacious and convenient entrance, was acquired by exchange June 7, 1927, a small grandstand was erected in the spring of 1924, and in March, 1926, the local taxpayers voted another appropriation for the purchase of a sizeable addition to the original plot.

"In the fall of 1933 the village authorities commenced the development of the property along more extensive lines as a Work Relief Project. Several additional parcels of land were acquired to enlarge the left field which had been somewhat short of regulation size. The entire site was graded, a new diamond of approved type built, the grounds fenced, and the entrance extensively landscaped . . . and on August 3, 1934, Doubleday Field was formally reopened with fitting ceremonies."

The National Baseball Museum and Hall of Fame is the
most recent development at Cooperstown. It is a substantial
fire-proof building designed especially for the purpose of
housing the collection reflecting the history and development
of the national game. The building is of Colonial design and imposing appearance, a fit place in which many important relics and records
of baseball have already been placed. Selections of immortals
for the Hall of Fame are made annually and those elected for
the honor are represented by bronze plaques hung promi-
nently on the walls. These plaques have been provided by
the National and American Leagues, and form a valuable
contribution.

All this is very fine, and the taxpayers of Cooperstown are
to be commended for their fine public spirit. There can be not
the slightest doubt that their development of Doubleday
Field and the erection of the Baseball Museum and Hall of
Fame were both done in the best of good faith.

But now that their position has been proved to be erroneous, what is to be done? We do not wonder at their hesitancy to let the old legend go. Their fair, historic village has
for twenty-five years basked in the sun of a warm and prosperous publicity. Must Cooperstown now forego this? The
choice must be made by the people of Cooperstown themselves.

It is a delicate matter, but the people of Cooperstown can
and must make their choice. It is our opinion that if Cooperstown accepts the findings of later research, acknowledges
that the Doubleday story is erroneous and tells the facts, as
they may be revealed through later and better research, all
will be well. There is no reason why the Museum should not

be maintained at Cooperstown. It was put up in good faith: but its governors must now act in good faith. It is the functions of a Museum to teach the truth. If the Museum should insist on the perpetuation of an error, it would invite a skepticism which would increase with the years and in the end would make the Museum a thing of ridicule.

Judge Kenesaw Mountain Landis, in his speech dedicating the Baseball Museum on June 12, 1939, made no claims on behalf of Doubleday. Rather, he placed the Museum in its right perspective. "But I should like," he said, "and I think all these immortals of baseball would agree with me—I should like to dedicate this Museum to all America, to lovers of good sportsmanship, healthy bodies and clean minds. For those are the principles of baseball. So it is to them, rather than to the few who have been honored here, that I propose to dedicate this shrine of sportsmanship." If the Baseball Museum can be made to serve the best interests of real sportsmanship, its continuation at Cooperstown will be justified. We hope it will do so. But high ideals cannot be maintained on a basis of deceit. Honesty is essential and the Doubleday tradition cannot be upheld as a kind of Santa Claus of baseball. We cannot but feel that those in authority at Cooperstown will let their idol go and in his place build a shrine that shall be an inspiration for American youth.

25. A Patron Saint of Baseball

IT SEEMS to be necessary to have a patron saint of baseball. An editorial in *The Sun*, New York, June 10th, 1939, reads as follows:

"Monday's birthday party for baseball at Cooperstown includes the dedication of the National Baseball Museum and Hall of Fame and the dedication of Doubleday Field with a pageant, 'The Cavalcade of Baseball.' The party marks the *further assimilation of a convenient, popular and harmless legend* that General Abner Doubleday invented baseball at Cooperstown one hundred years ago. Historians may be able to demonstrate that baseball was actually played much longer ago, that the very name of the game appeared in print much earlier than 1839, that the earliest rules for playing the game were taken over bodily from other games, but all such demonstration will be in vain. Baseball is an established American institution and as such *requires as firmly established a legend.* So the public will continue to take part in the *innocuous conspiracy* to give General Doubleday fame as the inventor of baseball and Cooperstown glory as the birthplace of the game. The game, meantime, passes its *legendary birthday* in vigorous health, secure in the affections of a nation, confident of constant renewal of strength through successive generations of Americans."

195

Undiluted sophistry! If the sports writers, for the purpose of dramatization, must have a popular hero upon whom to bestow laurels for the beginning of America's national game, why should it be necessary to concoct an entirely legendary figure. Or, worse yet, why confuse a perfectly good American patriot and historical figure who justly earned distinction during the Civil War with an unhistorical, legendary fame? Doubleday stands in no need of a fame unjustly pinned upon him. To insist upon the baseball legend is not to honor him but to discredit him. How can those who know the facts refrain from smiling knowingly at the mention of his name, if not from giving a tolerant chuckle of amusement when some innocent speaks it. Must teachers in our schools perpetuate a legend when they know better?

Of course a patron Saint, a symbolic figure, is a great convenience to those who must write of baseball. Well then, why not select Alexander J. Cartwright for the honor, as the one who contributed most to the origin of organized baseball as it is known in America today. Call him the "Father of Organized Baseball" and stay within the bounds of history. It is no disgrace to the City of New York to be called the birthplace of organized baseball. To Alexander J. Cartwright especially, because, according to Charles A. Peverelly, he "one day upon the field proposed a regular organization," but also to D. F. Curry, E. R. Dupignac, Jr., W. H. Tucker and W. R. Wheaton, and the other men who organized the Knickerbocker Club of New York in the year 1845 should go credit for first setting up a reasonably stable organization, and in particular for drawing up a set of rules which may justly be called the foundation of the *modern* American game.

26. Lacrosse

A FINAL word should be made on the game of lacrosse. At first it seems to be an exception to the theory of the common origin of ball games, and claims to an American Indian origin are strong. But lacrosse has a double association with old world customs, one extremely ancient, the other modern.

Most accounts of Indian "ball games"—and there are many —describe tribal customs of the eighteenth and nineteenth century. It is certain, however, that they are pre-historic, and it is to be expected that changes over so long a period might dim their original purpose. But in such comparatively recent descriptions as that of George Catlin, the Indian ball "games" are obviously more than games. They were played in "a serious manner," tribe against tribe, in struggles lasting a whole day. Long, careful preparations were made, with many rituals such as "going to the water," fasting and scarifying the limbs. Large numbers participated in the ceremonies which preceded the games, and in the actual games, which usually took place on certain anniversaries, as well as in the springtime. They were played with such ferocity that accidents occurred and limbs were frequently broken. The main feature of the

Indian game was a short stick with a net at one end (later called the crosse), with which the ball was thrown or carried to distant goals. There can be no doubt that these so-called games were originally, if not still are religious ceremonies. Their purpose was to ensure the strength, virility and manhood of the young players, and hence the perpetuation of the tribe.

American Indian ball rituals, 1838.

Was there a connection with the old world rites? The resemblance in idea and purpose is so great that one can well believe there is, and an examination of the available evidence leads to the conclusion that there is an historical continuity between the ancient Egyptian fertility rites and the American Indian ball games.

Then how did the customs get to America? They travelled in an easterly direction through India, Assam, Borneo and the islands of the Pacific, in all probability reaching the west coast of South America, at what is now Peru, and from there spreading northwards through Central America to the North American plains. The customs came with the people. This theory has been held by many archeologists. It has been ably presented by W. J. Perry in the chapter on *Archaic Civilization and its Spread* in his *The Growth of Civilization*. There is, sums up Perry, "a chain of communities from India to America, all possessing cultures strikingly similar, in all essentials, to that of Egypt in the Pyramid Age." Le Plongeon lists most convincingly a host of similarities between the Maya and Ancient Egyptian civilizations.

A characteristic feature of these migrating civilizations was the head-cults found even today in Assam, Borneo and throughout the Polynesian Islands. It is certain that in the Polynesian and other Pacific islands there has long been a belief that their rulers were "Divine Kings" whose heads possessed fertilizing properties such as we have seen in the old Egyptian dynasties.

One of the most remarkable instances of this is found at Easter Island. On that mysterious island, about a thousand miles west of Peru, crowded with relics of an extinct civilization, evidences exist showing that "all the people believed that the head of the king had the most marvellous fertilizing power . . . Even when dead, there was a struggle to get hold of the skull and mark it with a hieroglyph similar to that marked on the boundary stones as a sign and stimulus of fertility." A modern psychoanalyst, in an attempt to find the meaning of head hunting, insists that it was considered "essential to produce a high birth rate and abundant field crops . . . We cannot escape the conclusion that this ceremonial type of warfare is actually, directly perhaps, or indirectly

199

related symbolically to . . . pregnancy in women . . . So, too, this practice of head hunting serves to fertilize the fields."

When the trans-Pacific migrants, after many centuries, eventually reached the shores of South America, they imported their religious customs, one of which was their belief in the fertilizing head of their ruler. And just as this belief developed in the old world with a change to a ball as the head-like symbol of fertility, so we find it developed in the new world, as a series of fantastic myths and customs indicate.

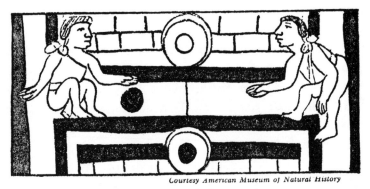

Courtesy American Museum of Natural History

Ancient Aztec ball game.

When the Spaniards came to Central America they found amongst the Aztecs and Mayas well established ball customs. The oldest reference to these is probably the story, recorded about the year 1550, by a Quiché Maya, although stone temples and carvings are testimony to a much older practice. The Quiché story concerns a head, used as a ball, which was the fertilizing agent resulting in the birth of the twins Hunahpu and Xbalanqui. J. Leslie Mitchell speaks of this story as being "in many ways a re-enactment of the oldest drama in the world, especially the incidents in the ball court.

That drama is the fight for and recovery of the body of Horus in Egyptian mythology . . . In later steps and other countries the body was dispensed with, and the symbol of the head used instead. From this arose all early ball games."

The famous Ball Court, part of the Temple of the Warriors in Chichen Itza, Yucatan, was the scene of the most important of the Maya ball ceremonies. It was two hundred and seventy two feet long, by one hundred and nineteen feet wide, surrounded by huge stone walls, most elaborately carved with religious figures. Two large stone rings, placed twenty feet above the ground, in the center of the longer sides, suggest that the game was played across the narrower width of the court. The soft rubber ball had to be butted, not thrown, from some part of the body, head, shoulder, hips, knee or elbow, through the rings.

The bas-reliefs around the court emphasize the religious significance of the ball-rites, but especially the importance of the head. The players were not ordinary people, but were of noble caste, probably priests. Seven on a side, they are shown each with a large flint knife in one hand, and a head in the other. Another figure shows a kneeling warrior whose severed head is held by a priest, while from his neck sprouts seven streams of blood in the form of serpents. "The whole probably represents," says Thomas Gann, "the fertilization of the earth by blood sacrifice to the earth god, and shows close connection between the ball game and the gods of fertility."

We have seen how the old game of *la soule*, in some places played with a *crosse*, was known in 1361 as *ad soulam crossare* and as *chouler á la crosse* in 1381. Later it was known as *crosserie*. It became the popular game of Brittany, where it was known in the seventeenth and eighteenth centuries as *jeu de la crosse.* When the French settled in Canada they noted a similarity between the Indian rites and their familiar game of *jeu de la crosse,* and promptly gave the French name to the Indian rite. Later the name was anglicised to *lacrosse.* Charlevoix, the French explorer, was perhaps the first to record the new name in 1744. Alexander Henry used the term in 1763.

A natural interest in the game led the French Canadians to experiment with the Indian form of the crosse with the small net, instead of the curved stick as used in France. The idea of picking up the ball in the crosse and throwing it was new to them. About the year 1839 there was a regularly organized lacrosse club at Montreal, which played matches with the Indians. It is reported that the Club succeeded in winning only one game, and it did not long survive. In 1856 the Iroquois Indians of Caughnawaga introduced lacrosse as a field sport, but it was not until 1860 that W. G. Beers, a Canadian attorney, published a brochure in which he attempted to reduce lacrosse to rules. Up to that time "it was barren of laws, and goalkeeper was the only player with a definite name and position." In 1859 Beers had proposed to make lacrosse the national game of Canada, and this was practically assured when a new Montreal Club, in 1867, revised Beers' rules and made them official.

It is evident, then, that lacrosse as played today is the result of a re-union of a stream of culture, rising in Ancient Egypt, breaking into two streams which flowed east and west around the world, until they meet again in the synthesis of the Indian ball game and the French *jeu de la crosse,* to make the modern game of lacrosse.

List of References

1. Aberdare, Lord, *Rackets, Squash Rackets, Tennis, Fives and Badminton*, pp. 20-21, 198-199 (London, 1933).

2. Al-Jahiz, "A Risala of Al-Jahiz," translated by J. Finkel, *American Oriental Society Journal*, vol. 47, p. 328 (New Haven, 1927).

3. Altham, H. S., *A History of Cricket* (London, 1926).

4. *Arabian Nights—The Thousand and One Nights*, "The Story of King Yoonan and the Sage Dooban." Lane Edition, vol. I, pp. 84-87 (London, 1839).

5. Augustine, Saint, *The Works* . . . "On Christian Doctrine," vol. IX, Book 4, Ch. 24, p. 163 (Edinburgh, 1873).

6. Austen, J., *Northanger Abbey*, p. 3 (London, 1851).

7. *Ball Player's Chronicle* (New York, 1867).

8. Barthelemey, A. de, "Récherches Historiques sur Quelques Droits et Redevances Bizarres au Moyen Age," *Revue de Bretagne et de Vendée*, Vol. VI, pp. 349-357 (Nantes, 1859).

9. Bede, *Ecclesiastical History*, Book 1, Ch. XXX, pp. 55-56 (London, 1849).

10. Beers, W. G., *Lacrosse, the National Game of Canada* (New York, 1869).

11. Beleth, J., "Rationale Divinorum Officiorum." In: Migne, J. P., *Patrologiae Cursus Completus*, Ser. 2, Vol. 202, Ch. 120 (Paris, 1855).

12. Belknap, G. N., "The Social Value of the Dionysiac Ritual," *Revue de l'Histoire des Religions*, Vol. 106, pp. 575-591 (Paris, 1932).

13. Bennett, J., *Billiards* (London, 1873).

14. Bimbinet, E., "Justice du Chapitre de Sainte-Croix," *Societé*

Archéologique et Historique de l'Orléanais. Mémoires, Vol. 6, pp. 143-146 (Orléans, 1863).

15. Birdsall, R., *The Story of Cooperstown,* pp. 224-230 (Cooperstown, 1917).

16. Blackman, W. S., "Fertility Rites in Modern Egypt," *Discovery,* Vol. 3, pp. 154-158 (London, 1922).

17. Bodleian Library, *Douce Mss.* 62, f. 143; 135, f. 7; 264, ff. 22, 44, 63.

18. Bourne, H., *Antiquitates Vulgares,* Ch. 24 (London, 1725).

19. Boutillier, L'Abbé, "Drames Liturgiques et Rites Figurés, Ou, Cérémonies Symbologiques dans l'Église de Nevers," *Société Nivernaise des Sciences, Lettres et Arts. Bulletin,* Ser. 2, Vol. 8, pp. 510-515 (Nevers, 1880).

20. Boutillier, L'Abbé, "Les Jeux de Paume à Nevers," *Société Nivernais des Sciences, Lettres et Arts. Bulletin,* Ser. 3, Vol. 2, pp. 5-12 (Nevers, 1884).

21. *Boy's Book of Sports,* pp. 11-12 (New Haven, 1839).

22. *Boys and Girls Book of Sports,* pp. 18-19 (Providence, R. I., 1835).

23. Bradford, W., *History of Plymouth Plantation,* p. 126 (New York, 1908).

24. Brand, J., *Observations on Popular Antiquities,* Vol. 1, pp. 70-72 (London, 1883).

25. Brown, J. M., *The Riddle of the Pacific,* pp. 76-77 (London, 1924).

26. Buchanan, J., *The Games of Lawn Tennis and Badminton,* p. 104 (London, 1876).

27. Burke, W. R. *A History of Spain,* p. 170 (New York, 1900).

28. Cady, A. H., *Billiards,* pp. 4-6 (New York, 1896).

29. Carew, R., *The Survey of Cornwall,* pp. 74-75 (London, 1602).

30. Carré, H., *Jeux, Sports et Divertissements des Rois de France,* p. 92 (Paris, 1937).

31. Carver, R., *The Book of Sports,* pp. 37-40 (Boston, 1834).

32. Catlin, G., *Illustrations of the Manners, Customs and Condition of the North American Indians* (London, 1848).

33. *Children's Amusements,* p. 9 (New York, 1820).

34. Cinnamus, J., *De Rebus Gestis,* pp. 186-187 (Trajecti ad Rhenum, 1652). Quoted in: Whitman, p. 159.

35. Clark, R., *Golf: A Royal and Ancient Game,* pp. x-xi (London, 1893).

36. Clarke, W., *The Boy's Own Book*, pp. 20-21 (London, 1829, also Boston, 1829).

37. Clifford, W. G., *Billiards Through the Centuries* (London, 1933).

38. Cochard, L'Abbé, "Le Jeu de Paume à Orléans," *Société Archéologique et Historique de l'Orléanais. Mémoires*, Vol. 22, pp. 297-340 (Orléans, 1889). Also published separately.

39. Collender, H. W., *Modern Billiards*, p. 3 (New York, 1881).

40. Cotton, C., *The Compleat Gamester*, frontis., (London, 1674).

41. Crawley, A. E., *Technique of Lawn Tennis*, p. 8 (London, 1923).

42. Crooke, W., "Legends of Krishna," *Folk-Lore*, Vol. 11, pp. 20-21 (London, 1900).

43. Culin, S., *Games of the North American Indians*, pp. 561 ff. (Washington, D. C., 1907).

44. Dale, T. F., *The Game of Polo*, pp. 2-3 (London, 1897).

45. Darlington, H. S., "The Meaning of Headhunting," *Psychoanalytic Review*, Vol. 26, pp. 55-68 (New York, 1939).

46. Dexter, T. F. G., *Fire Worship in Britain*, pp. 39-40 (London, 1931).

47. Doutté, E., *Merrakech*, pp. 322-324 (Paris, 1905).

48. Du Cange, *Glossarium Mediae et Infimae Latinatis*, Vol. 4: Mellat, Vol. 5: Pelota (Paris, 1846).

49. Duine, F., *Bréviares et Missels des Églises et Abbayes Brétonnes*, p. 35 (Rennes, 1906). Quoted in: Gougaud, p. 579.

50. Dunbar, W., "Devorit With Dreme," *Poems*, p. 83 (Edinburgh, 1893).

51. Durandus, G., *Rationale Divinorum Officiorum*, Book VI, Ch. 86, Sect. 9 (Rome, 1473).

52. D'Urfey, *Wit and Mirth, Or, Pills to Purge Melancholy*, Vol. 1, p. 91 (London, 1719).

53. Effler, L. R., *The Ruins of Chichen Itza*, pp. 19-21 (Toledo, O., 1936).

54. *Encyclopedia Britannica*, "Athena," Vol. 2, p. 829 (New York, 1910).

55. *Encyclopedia Britannica*, "Spain," Vol. 25, p. 541 (New York, 1911).

56. *Encyclopedia of Canada*, "Lacrosse," Vol. 3, p. 371 (Toronto, 1936).

57. Ewing, G., *The Military Journal of George Ewing (1754-1824)*, *A Soldier of Valley Forge*, pp. 35, 47 (Yonkers, N. Y., 1928).

58. *Female Robinson Crusoe*, *A Tale of the American Wilderness*, pp. 176-178 (New York, 1837).

59. Fessenden, T. G., *The Complete Farmer and Rural Economist*, Advertising leaves (Boston, 1834).

60. *The First Lie; or, Falsehood its Own Punishment* (New Haven, 1835).

61. Fitzstephen, quoted in: J. Stow, *A Survey of London*, p. 214 (London, 1892).

62. Florio, J., *A Worlde of Wordes*, under: "Sgrillare" (London, 1598).

63. Frazer, Sir J. G., *The Golden Bough*, Vol. 9, "The Scapegoat," (London, 1925).

64. Gann, T., *Glories of the Maya*, pp. 250-251 (New York, 1939).

65. Géraud, H., "Paris Sous Phillipe Le Bel," *Le Livre de la Taille de Paris pour l'An 1292*, pp. 1-179 (Paris, 1837).

66. Giles, H. A., "Football and Polo in China," *Nineteenth Century*, Vol. 59, pp. 508-509 (London, 1906).

67. Gini, C., "Rural Ritual Games in Libya," *Rural Sociology*, Vol. 4, pp. 283-299 (University, La., 1939).

68. Glave, E. J., "The Slave Trade in The Congo," *The Century Magazine*, Vol. 39, pp. 827-828 (New York, 1890).

69. Godard-Faultrier, *Société d'Agriculture, Science et Arts d'Angers. Mémoires*, Ser. 2, Vol. 5, p. 157. Quoted in: Barthelemey, pp. 351, 579.

70. Gouberville, G. P., *Journal Manuscrit du Sire de Gouberville*. Publiée partiellement par l'Abbé Tollmer, Vol. 1, pp. 173-174 (Paris, 1879).

71. Gougaud, L., "La Soule en Bretagne," *Annales de Bretagne*, Vol. 27, pp. 571-604 (Paris, 1911).

72. Grantham, W. W., *Stoolball* (London, 1919).

73. Grimm, J., *Teutonic Mythology* (London, 1880-1888). Quoted in: Dexter, pp. 39-40.

74. Guiffrey, J. M. J., *Les Amours de Gombaut et de Macée* (Paris, 1882).

75. Guillim, J., *A Display of Heraldry*, Sect. 4, pp. 321, 325 (London, 1724).

76. Haswell, C. H., *Reminiscences of an Octogenarian of the City of New York*, p. 427 (New York, 1896).

77. Henderson, R. W., "Moses Provençal on Tennis," *Jewish Quarterly Review*, Vol. 26, pp. 1-6 (Philadelphia, 1935).

78. *Herodotus* with an English translation by A. D. Godley. Book I, c. 94, Book IV, c. 180 (New York, 1921).

79. Hervey, Lady Mary Lepell, *Letters*, p. 139 (London, 1821).

80. Heywood, J. "The Playe Called Foure P. P.," *The Dramatic Writings*, p. 54 (London, 1905).

81. Hickey, W., *Memoirs*, Vol. 1, pp. 72-73 (New York, 1921).

82. Hilton, H. H., and G. G. Smith, *The Royal and Ancient Game of Golf* (London, 1912).

83. Hilton-Simpson, H. W., *Among the Hill Folk of Algeria*, p. 88 (London, 1921).

84. *Historical Gossip About Golf and Golfers: By a Golfer*, p. 2 (Edinburgh, 1863).

85. Hone, P., *The Diary of Philip Hone*, pp. 757, 773, 842 (New York, 1927).

86. Howell, J., *Instructions for Forreine Travell*, p. 20 (London, 1642).

87. Howlett, R., *School for Recreation*, pp. 96-98 (London, 1696).

88. Hubert, H., and M. Mauss, "Essai sur le Sacrifice," *L'Année Sociologique*, Vol. 2, p. 109 (Paris, 1898).

89. Hughes, C. E., "The History of Billiards in Pictures," *Fry's Magazine*, Vol. 2, pp. 403-413 (London, 1905).

90. "Humours of The Fleet, Written by a Gentleman of the College" (London, 1740). Quoted in: J. Ashton, *The Fleet* (New York, 1888).

91. Hutchinson, H. G., *Golf* (London, 1902).

92. Jeakes, T. J., "Cornish Hurling," *Notes and Queries*, Ser. 8, Vol. 11, pp. 510-511 (London, 1897).

93. *Jeux des Jeunes Garçons* (Paris, c. 1810, also 1822).

94. Johnson, W. B., "Football a Survival of Magic?" *Contemporary Review*, Vol. 135, pp. 225-231 (London, 1929).

95. Julyan, W. L., "Cornwall's Annual Hurling Matches," *The Field*, Vol. 187, p. 244 (London, 1946).

96. Jusserand, J. J., *Les Sports et Jeux d'Exercice dans l'Ancienne France*, Chapter VI: Paume, Soule, Crosse (Paris, 1901).

97. Knickerbocker Base Ball Club, *Game Books*. Mss. in The New York Public Library.

98. Krappe, A. H., *The Science of Folk-lore*, pp. 272 ff. (London, 1930).

99. La Bedollière, E., *Moeurs et Vie Privée des Français dans les Premiéres Siècles de la Monarchie*, Vol. 3, pp. 377-380 (Paris, 1835).

100. La Borderie, A. de, "Géographie Féodale: Seigneurie de Rochfort," *Mèlanges d'Histoire et d'Archéologie Bretonnes*, Vol. 1, p. 100. Quoted in: Gougaud, p. 579.

101. Latham, W., *The Diary*. Quoted in: W. C. Bronson, *The History of Brown University*, p. 245 (Providence, R. I., 1914).

102. Leaf, W., *Walter Leaf: Some Chapters of Autobiography*, pp. 74-75 (London, 1932).

103. Leber, C., *Collection des Meilleurs Dissertations*, Vol. 9, pp. 391-401 (Paris, 1826-1838).

104. Leo Africanus, "The History and Description of Africa," *Hakluyt Society. Publications*, Vol. 93, pp. 454-455 (London, 1896).

105. Le Plongeon, A., *Vestiges of the Mayas* (New York, 1881).

106. Lindsay, Sir D., "The Complaynt," *The Works . . .* Scottish Text Society. *Publications*, Ser. 3, Vol. 1, pp. 39-53, Vol. 3, pp. 46-64 (Edinburgh, 1931).

107. *Little Pretty Pocket-Book, Intended for the Instruction and Amusement of Little Master Tommy and Pretty Miss Polly* (London, 1744, also New York, 1860; London, 1767; Philadelphia, 1786; Worcester, 1787. No copies known of 1744, 1760 and 1786 editions).

108. Luce, S., *La France Pendant la Guerre de Cent Ans*, Vol. 1, pp. 112-127 (Paris, 1890).

109. Luze, A. de, "Le Jeu de Paume, Jeu National Francais," *Revue de Paris, Année* 37, Vol. 6, p. 349 (Paris, 1930).

110. Luze, A de, *La Magnifique Histoire du Jeu de Paume* (Paris, 1933).

111. Macdonald, A., "Shinty: Historical and Traditional," *Gaelic Society of Inverness. Transactions*, Vol. 30, p. 32 (Inverness, 1919-1922).

112. Macdonald, C. B., *Scotland's Gift: Golf* (New York, 1928).

113. Macdonald, J. N., *Shinty: A Short History of The Ancient Highland Game* (Inverness, 1932).

114. Magoun, F. P., Jr., "Shrove Tuesday Football," *Harvard Studies and Notes in Philology and Literature*, Vol. 12, pp. 9-46 (Cambridge, 1931).

115. Mannhardt, W., *Wald- und Feldkulte*, Vol. 1, pp. 471-480 (Berlin, 1875).

116. Massingham, H. J., "Origins of Ball Games," In: *The Heritage of Man*, pp. 208-227 (London, 1929).

117. Matthews, J. H., *A History of the Parishes of Saint Ives, Lelant, Towednack and Zennor*, pp. 393-394 (London, 1892).

118. Mercier, L. C. E., *La Chasse et les Sports Chez les Arabes*, p. 177 (Paris, 1927).

119. Middleton, T., "Father Hubburd's Tales." *The Works* . . . pp. 102-103 (London, 1885).

120. Mirk, J., "Instructions to Parish Priests," *Early English Text Society*, Old Series 31, p. 11 (London, 1868).

121. Mitchell, J. L., *The Conquest of the Maya* (New York, 1935).

122. Monckton, O. P., *Pastimes in Times Past*, pp. 117-138 (London, 1913).

123. Moor, E., *Suffolk Words and Phrases*, p. 238 (Woodbridge, 1823).

124. Moret, A., *La Mise à Mort du Dieu en Egypt*, p. 8 (Paris, 1927).

125. Moret, A., "Rituels Agraires de l'Ancien Orient à la Lamière des Nouveaux Textes des Ras Shamra," *Annuaire de l'Institut de Philologie et d'Histoire Orientales. Université Libre de Bruxelles*, Vol. 3, pp. 311-342 (Brussels, 1935).

126. Morice, H., *Mémoires Pour Servir de Preuves à l'Histoire Ecclésiastique et Civile de Bretagne*, Vol. 2, cols. 1284-1285 (Paris, 1744).

127. Naville, E., "The Temple of Deir el Bahari," *Egyptian Exploration Fund. Memoirs*, Vol. 19, part IV, plate C (London, 1901).

128. *New Book of Sports*, pp. 84-85 (London, 1885).

129. *New York Primer: or, Second Book*, Woodcut on back cover (New York, 1823).

130. P. -T., H., *Early Cricket. . . and Some Comments on Creag', Criquet, Cricce and Shakespeare's Clue* (Nottingham, 1923).

131. "Pastime of Racket," *The Sun* (New York, May 7, 1876).

132. Perry, W. J., "Archaic Civilization and its Spread," *The Growth of Civilization*, pp. 76-111 (London, 1924).

133. Peverelly, C. A., *The Book of American Pastimes*, p. 338 (New York, 1866).

134. Pezron, P., *The Antiquities of the Nations: More Particularly of the Celtae*, pp. 200-201 (London, 1706).

135. Pigeon, L'Abbé E. A., *La Diocese d' Avranches*, Vol. 1, pp. 113-114 (Coutances, 1888). Quoted in: Luce, p. 119.

136. Pix, M., *The Double Distress*, Prologue (London, 1701).

137. Poitiers, *L'Armorial des Maires de Poitiers (1213-1676)*. Coté 20084.

138. *Popular Pastimes: Being a Selection of Picturesque Representations of the Customs and Amusements of Great Britain* (London, 1816).

139. Prior, R. C. A., *Notes on Croquet and Some Other Ancient Bat and Ball Games Related to It*. Translation of "The Game of Chicane," from Du Cange, p. 5-13 (London, 1872).

140. Racket Court Club, *Constitution and By-Laws* (New York, 1845).

141. Racket Court Club, *By-Laws* (New York, 1853).

142. Racket Court Club, *Members* (New York, 1846).

143. Richter, F. C., *Richter's History and Records of Baseball*, pp. 12-13, 17-31 (Philadelphia, 1914).

144. Roberts, P., *The Cambrian Popular Antiquities*, pp. 110-111, 123, 333 (London, 1815).

145. St. John, J. A., *The History of the Manners and Customs of Ancient Greece*, Vol. 1, p. 157 (London, 1842).

146. Smith, H., *Festivals, Games and Amusements, Ancient and Modern*, p. 330 (New York, 1831).

147. Souvestre, E., *Les Derniers Bretons*, Vol. 1, pp. 125-132 (Paris, 1858).

148. Stewart, J. L., *Golfiana Miscellanea*, p. 11 (London, 1887).

149. "Stool-ball, or, The Easter Diversion," *London Magazine*, Vol. 2, pp. 637-638 (London, 1733).

150. Strutt, J., *The Sports and Pastimes of the People of England* (London, 1801).

151. Tabari, *Geschichte der Perser und Araber*, übersetzt . . . von T. Nöldeke, p. 29 (Leyden, 1879).

152. Tafur, P., *Travels and Adventures, 1435-1439*, pp. 80, 240 (London, 1926).

153. Taylor, J., "A Short Relation of a Long Journey," *Works* . . . p. 23 (London, 1872).

154. Vergil, P., *A Pleasant and Compendious History of the First Inventors* (London, 1702).

155. Vic, C., and J. J. Vaissete, *Histoire Général du Languedoc*, Vol. 2. Preuves, col. 518 (Paris, 1733).

156. Vienne, "Manuscrit de l'Église de Vienne," *Mercure de France*, p. 475 (Paris, March, 1727).

157. Ward, J. M., *Base-ball: How to Become a Player*, pp. 12-21 (New York, 1888).

158. Watts, H. E., *The Christian Recovery of Spain*, p. 6 (New York, 1894).

159. Weed, T., *Autobiography*, Vol. 1, p. 203 (Boston, 1883).

160. Welsh, C., *A Bookseller of the Last Century . . . John Newbery*, p. 293 (London, 1885).

161. Wentworth, Lady, *Thoroughbred Racing Stock* (London, 1938). Chapter IX: "Tchigan, the Origin of Tennis." First published in *The Field*, Vol. 150, pp. 740-741 (London, 1927).

162. Westermarck, E. A., *Ritual and Belief in Morocco*, Vol. 2, pp. 271-272 (London, 1926).

163. Whitman, M. D., *Tennis Origins and Mysteries*, With an Historical Bibliography by Robert W. Henderson, pp. 95-102 (New York, 1932).

164. Whitney, C. W., "The Racquet and Tennis Club of New York," *Harper's Weekly*, Vol. 37, pp. 155, 158-159 (New York, 1893).

165. Wilde, Lady J. F. E., *Ancient Cures, Charms and Usages of Ireland*, pp. 101-102 (London, 1890).

166. Wingfield, W. C., *The Major's Game of Lawn Tennis. By W. C. W.* (London, November 1873). Cover title: *Sphairistike or Lawn Tennis*.

167. Woodruff, C. H., "Origin of Cricket," *Baily's Magazine*, Vol. 6, p. 51 (London, 1901).

Index

Footnotes have been omitted from the text of this book, but citations may be found by means of this index. Numbers in italics refer to the corresponding numbered item in the *List of References*.

Vermandais, 41:*108*
Vexin Normand, 41:*108*
Vienne, 37:*48, 99*
Vieux-Pont, 82:*115*
Vigne, H. de, 122:*28, 39*
Vitré, ball ceremonies, 46:*49*

Wales, knappan. See: Knappan
Walton, I., 62
Ward, J. M., 171, 175, 178
Warriors, Temple of, 201:*64*
Webster, J., 65, 66

Weed, T., 146, 161
Wentworth, Lady, 32:*161*
Westermarck, E. A., 24:*162*
Wheaton, W. R., 162, 196
Whitman, M. D., 127:*163*
Wilson, Rev. T., 132:*167*
Wingfield, Major W. C., 125:*41*
Worcester, Mass., baseball, 150

Xbalanqui, 200:*121*

Yule 35:*73*

University of Illinois Press
1325 South Oak Street
Champaign, IL 61820-6903
www.press.uillinois.edu